I0644665

LEADERSHIP

Leadership: The Basics provides an easy, jargon-free introduction to the fundamentals of leadership and leadership theory.

Strongly grounded in research and engaging with the key theories, this book explains the key aspects of leadership including:

- Different types of leadership such as servant leadership, transformational leadership and situational leadership
- Ethics
- Diversity
- Dark leadership
- Leadership in practice
- Common models of leadership

This book provides an accessible and engaging introduction to leadership, making it perfect for undergraduate students enrolled in leadership courses. It also serves as an excellent starting point for anyone seeking to deepen their understanding of leadership.

Morgen Witzel is an internationally known writer and lecturer on leadership, management and ethics.

The Basics

The Basics is a highly successful series of accessible guidebooks which provide an overview of the fundamental principles of a subject area in a jargon-free and undaunting format.

Intended for students approaching a subject for the first time, the books both introduce the essentials of a subject and provide an ideal springboard for further study. With over 50 titles spanning subjects from artificial intelligence (AI) to women's studies, *The Basics* are an ideal starting point for students seeking to understand a subject area.

Each text comes with recommendations for further study and gradually introduces the complexities and nuances within a subject.

PUBLIC HEALTH
FIONA SIM AND JENNY WRIGHT

SENECA
CHRISTOPHER V. TRINACTY

GLOBAL COMICS
FREDERICK LUIS ALDAMA

CONTEMPORARY INDIA
REKHA DATTA

POLYGAMY
BRUCE WHITEHOUSE AND WILLIAM JANKOWIAK

SUICIDE
MATIAS GAY

ROMANTICISM
ELIZABETH A. FAY

LEADERSHIP
MORGEN WITZEL

For more information about this series, please visit: www.routledge.com/The-Basics/book-series/B

LEADERSHIP

THE BASICS

Morgen Witzel

Routledge
Taylor & Francis Group
LONDON AND NEW YORK

Designed cover image: Getty Images

First published 2027
by Routledge
4 Park Square, Milton Park, Abingdon, Oxon OX14 4RN

and by Routledge
605 Third Avenue, New York, NY 10158

Routledge is an imprint of the Taylor & Francis Group, an informa business

British Library Cataloguing-in-Publication Data
A catalogue record for this book is available from the British Library

Library of Congress Cataloging-in-Publication Data
Names: Witzel, Morgen author
Title: Leadership: the basics / Morgen Witzel.
Description: Abingdon, Oxon; New York, NY: Routledge, 2027. |
Series: The basics | Includes bibliographical references and index.
Identifiers: LCCN 2026016858 (print) | LCCN 2026016859 (ebook) |
ISBN 9781032802930 hardback | ISBN 9781032802848 paperback |
ISBN 9781003496243 ebook
Subjects: LCSH: Leadership
Classification: LCC HM1261 .W58 2027 (print) | LCC HM1261 (ebook)
LC record available at https://lccn.loc.gov/2026016858
LC ebook record available at https://lccn.loc.gov/2026016859

ISBN: 9781032802930 (hbk)
ISBN: 9781032802848 (pbk)
ISBN: 9781003496243 (ebk)

DOI: 10.4324/9781003496243

Typeset in Bembo
by Deanta Global Publishing Services, Chennai, India

CONTENTS

LIST OF FIGURES

LIST OF TABLES

1

AN INTRODUCTION TO LEADERSHIP

In January 2026, a search on Amazon.com for books with 'leadership' in the title brought up over seventy thousand results. The number of journal articles, newspaper columns, blog posts, TED Talks and other videos is beyond counting. The question can be fairly asked: why write yet another book about leadership?

The answer comes in two parts. First, the sheer volume of writing and speaking about leadership reminds us of how omnipresent leadership is. It affects so many aspects of our daily lives, in our places of work and worship, in our social lives, even in our homes. Across these different domains, leadership manifests itself in many ways. It can be a force for inspiration or a tool for domination – or both. It can be driver of change, a force for consolidation or a means of reinforcing permanence. It can stem from personal ambition, or it can have its roots in a desire to be of service and to help others. In short, leadership can be almost anything that we want it to be – and sometimes, when leadership oppresses or abuses us, it can be things we don't want it to be.

Second, a lot of writing about leadership starts from the premise that if we can define what leadership is, we can break it down into its component parts and create a recipe for good leadership. This is understandable, because many people in positions of leadership struggle to define what leadership is and to get better at it. Writers and speakers have tried to identify principles of good

DOI: 10.4324/9781003496243-1

leadership, the logic being that if we follow those principles, we ourselves will become good leaders.

When studying leadership, though, rational logic only takes us so far. If there is one thing that we have learned from all those thousands of studies and observations, it is that leadership is very hard to pin down and define. That in turn makes it hard to study and analyse. We can observe the ways that leaders behave, the techniques that they use in their attempts to influence or control others, and we can see how other people respond to these attempts, but these don't really capture what leadership itself actually *is*.

Many attempts have been made to define leadership. This example comes from management consultants McKinsey & Company, who have a lot of experience in the field and should know a thing or two. 'Leadership', they say, 'is a set of mindsets and behaviors that aligns people in a collective direction, enables them to work together and accomplish shared goals, and helps them adjust to changing environments.'

This is a good start, but it doesn't tell us what those mindsets and behaviours are, or why this enables people to work together (or why they would want to work together). That's because those necessary mindsets and behaviours will often be quite different: an approach to leadership that works well in one culture or organisation might fail disastrously when transplanted to another. The reasons why people work together differ too, depending on who they are and where they are.

Other definitions treat leadership as a static process, something that can be broken down into convenient steps: define a clear vision, engage people, communicate a clear message and so on. The implication is that if we do all of these steps in order, joining the dots, we will have leadership. But as anyone who has ever tried to lead an organisation in practice will tell you, the reality is not that simple.

The mere fact that so much has been written and said about leadership – those seventy thousand Amazon results are just the tip of the iceberg – complicates the picture still further and makes it harder to define what leadership is. The foundational texts and stories of nearly every civilisation feature leadership as a common theme. Here are a few examples:

- The *Bhagavad Gita*, composed in India sometime between the second and fourth centuries BC, is in part a meditation on the nature of a leader's duties;
- The *Iliad*, written in ancient Greek and dating probably from the sixth century BC, has been described as a critique of leadership, showing what happens when leaders put their own interests ahead of those who follow them;
- The *Epic of Gilgamesh*, composed on clay tablets sometime around 1800 BC, portrays the leader as a wise and all-knowing figure;
- *The Duties of the Vizier*, written on papyrus in the early sixteenth century BC, sets out the duties of a leader in practical terms;
- The *Huangdi Neijing*, compiled in China in the first or second century BC, depicts the legendary first emperor of China, Huangdi, as being a great source of knowledge and wisdom.

These and many other works like them portray leaders as gods and heroes, with the result that for many centuries we believed that leaders had to be godlike and heroic. Sometime around the tenth century AD in Europe and Asia there emerged a genre of works known as 'mirrors for princes', guidebooks advising kings and princes on how to rule their domains. Later came the fashion for biographies of 'great' leaders like Napoleon Bonaparte, Frederick II of Prussia, Tsarina Catherine of Russia and so on; by the end of the nineteenth century, biographies of powerful business leaders also began to emerge. There was a long debate about what 'greatness' is: for the British scholar Thomas Carlyle, for example, 'greatness' was indicated by how well a leader responds in times of adversity, and how they overcome the barriers placed before them.

Even today there is a tendency to think of leaders as being somehow superior to the rest of us, more powerful, more intelligent, more perceptive; more of whatever it takes to be a leader. This assumption misses two key points: (1) all leaders are fallible and all make mistakes, so much so that the careers of powerful leaders often end in disaster; and (2) most leadership is not heroic. Most leaders do their work quietly and are rarely recognised outside their immediate environment. Along with the heroic tradition of leadership, there is another less well-known strain of thinking which says that the best leaders are the ones who remain in the background and enable other people to get on with their work and lives. For example, the *Daodejing* (*Tao Te Ching*), compiled in China in the fourth century BC, calls on leaders to be self-effacing and not interfere directly in the lives of their subjects.

Put simply, leadership is not always what we think it is. In this book, we will not even try to define what leadership *is*, because the breadth of the subject and the variety of approaches to leadership make this impossible. What we will do instead is look at issues that are common across leadership in all of its forms. These are the 'basics', things that everyone interested in leadership – whether as a student of the subject, as someone with the intention of becoming a leader or even someone who is already in a position of leadership – needs to consider.

Rather than trying (and failing) to come up with a single definition, let us instead use a classic investigation technique, the 5W1H method. This consists of asking six questions: *what*, *why*, *who*, *when*, *where* and *how*. Each question enables us to approach leadership from a different angle.

We start with the *what* question. Partly because of that emphasis on the godly and heroic, a number of misconceptions about leadership have gained common currency. There are also some things that will be true about leadership in most situations, most of the time. Some of these things are a matter of common sense, but you may feel that some of the others are counter-intuitive. There are a lot of paradoxes in leadership, apparent contradictions that we can never really resolve, and this is a running theme throughout this book.

MISCONCEPTIONS ABOUT LEADERSHIP

- *Leadership is only found at the top of the organisation.* When we think about leadership we often think only of the people at the top: the kings, presidents and prime ministers, the chief executives and chairs of businesses, the generals and admirals, the managers and captains of sports teams and so on. This is untrue. Even small organisations will have multiple leaders, people to whom others turn when they need help to get something done, for reassurance and advice, to get permission for something they want to do, or for any of a variety of other reasons. Big organisations will have hundreds of leaders, even thousands, scattered throughout the organisation.

- *Leaders control everything in their domain.* In fact, leaders directly control very little beyond their immediate environment. In big organisations, leaders rely on techniques such as coordination and influence to get things done, and (as we shall see later in this book) this involves a two-way dialogue between leaders and followers. The idea that leaders directly control the organisations they lead is a myth.
- *Leadership is inherent in some people but not others.* The historic notion that 'leaders are born, not made' continues to persist, but it is false. There is no leadership gene, no set of predetermined factors that means some people are pre-destined to lead. It is true that not everyone wants to become a leader, particularly at the highest level: some people lack the confidence to lead, others lack the ambition to do so, but this is as much a matter of personal mindset and desire as anything else. Training, mentoring and practice can all help people learn to lead, even if they have no prior experience of doing so.
- *Leaders must be charismatic.* Some leaders do have a great deal of charisma and are able to persuade people to follow them through force of personality. Others are quiet and lead by example, setting a standard that they hope others will follow. Because these leaders don't make a fuss or attract attention to themselves, we know less about them and it is easy to forget that they exist. Brash, outspoken leaders make headlines, but they also sometimes exhibit qualities of psychopathy and narcissism that makes them dangerous and can lead them and their followers into disaster.
- *Leadership skills are transferable, so a good leader will always be a good leader even if they move to a different organisation.* There are examples of leaders who are successful in more than one sector or field of activity, but there are also examples of leaders

with a track record of success who move on to new organisations and fail. Far from using the same approach and style of leadership everywhere, leaders who succeed in different organisations and domains tend to do so because they are able to adapt to their surroundings and change their approach.

- *Being a leader means that everyone else should obey you.* This implies that followers have a duty to comply with the leader's orders. This is known as 'legitimate authority' and is often enshrined in laws or contracts between leaders and followers. However, this also implies that leaders are always right, which is not true. There are times when it is necessary and essential to challenge the leaders. Leaders must be held to account, and we will discuss this further when we come to talk about governance.
- *People always want to be led.* This is controversial. It suits leaders to assume this, of course, and there will always be some people who lack confidence, experience or skills and want someone else to guide them. At the other end of the spectrum are highly skilled and confident people who know what needs to be done – probably better than their leaders do – and want to be left to get on with it. For these people, leaders are interfering busybodies who slow them down. As the *Daodejing* puts it, 'the highest type of leadership is that of which the people are unaware.'
- *Success is always down to good leadership.* Again, it suits leaders to think this, and when things go well someone in leadership is likely to step up and claim credit. However, a moment's thought tells us that leaders on their own cannot actually achieve very much. They need the hands and minds and hearts of other people to help them achieve their goals. Even if the leader provides the original idea or inspiration, successful outcomes are the result of cooperation and collaboration between leaders and followers. The same is true, of course, of failure.
- *Good leaders are always winners.* We are quick to condemn leaders when they fail, but all leaders fail at some time or another. Unfortunately, the stigma associated with failure means that leaders will sometimes go to extraordinary lengths, including unethical and illegal actions, to avoid failing, or at least, to avoid being *seen* to fail. Leaders are human beings, and failure is a part of life.

TRUTHS ABOUT LEADERSHIP

- *Anyone can find themselves in a position where they are a leader.* Some people are identified as having leadership potential and are trained and promoted into leadership roles, but others are 'accidental leaders'. They never set out to be leaders and had no ambitions in that direction, but they find themselves in positions of leadership nonetheless. Sometimes this is because another leader has departed and they have to step in to fill the gap, or sometimes it is because they have skills or experience that other leaders lack. We referred above to legitimate authority, but there are also other kinds of authority that can push people into positions of leadership.
- *Leadership requires people to take responsibility for their actions.* Leaders sometimes have to do hard things: things that will make them unpopular with other people, things that will challenge their own consciences and beliefs, or things that will do both. Leaders also need to take risks, with consequences that could be harmful to both themselves and the rest of the organisation. Making these decisions and living with the consequences is part of leadership. One of the reasons why people decline or avoid leadership positions is that they are not comfortable with that level of responsibility.
- *Leaders can't control everything.* If leaders *could* control everything around them, they could reduce the levels of risk they face, but they can't. The illusion of control is one of the most common fallacies in leadership, but as we noted above, in reality leaders control very little. They are heavily reliant on other people to get things done. This in turn adds another level of risk, because the leader doesn't always know whether those other people are doing what they should be doing, and usually the leader only finds out about problems when it is too late.
- *Leadership includes learning from failure.* Part of leadership is accepting the inevitability of failure and learning from it. Mistakes will happen, but thorough and honest post-mortem examinations can provide valuable learning that will help those mistakes from being repeated.
- *Leaders need to share power.* When we think of leadership we often think of powerful people using their power to get things

> done. However, as noted above, leaders have only a limited span of control and they have very little power outside of that control. In order to achieve their goals, therefore, leaders need to share power with their followers, enabling them to do what is required to reach that goal. As we will see, the more power a leader has, the more important it is that they share that power.

The last point brings up another important issue: the nature of power. When we think about power (and again this is partly because of past conditioning) we imagine it in terms of might and strength. Powerful leaders are those who have the ability to dominate others and compel them to do what the leader wants them to do. But this kind of power is very complex and requires the participation of a lot of other people to enforce the leader's will. The commander-in-chief of an army may seem to be a very powerful person, but they can do very little without the willing participation of their soldiers. If the soldiers refuse to obey orders, the leader is powerless.

True power is the ability to get things done by bringing other people together and combining their efforts. Charisma and personal strength can be sources of power, but they are not the only ones. Kindness and humility, even love, can also be forms of power because they create an environment where people trust their leaders and follow them willingly. Leaders need to take account of this.

THE PURPOSE OF LEADERSHIP

Why do leaders lead? Why is leadership necessary – or is it necessary at all? Does accepting leadership mean that we are surrendering part of our freedom? Thomas Jefferson, third president of the USA, once wrote that accepting direction and control from others 'is the last degradation of a free and moral agent.' Philosophical anarchists have argued that leadership is a form of tyranny. True leadership, they say, comes from the collective will of the people. Communities decide what is best for themselves, rather than inviting others to take charge.

This sounds attractive in theory, but in practice things rarely work this way. Studies of organisations and communities without leaders show that in nearly every case leaders emerge anyway. Sometimes they are promoted from within the group, or sometimes they are invited in from outside. The USA is an interesting case in point. The American colonies won their independence from Britain in 1783, but no president was immediately appointed. People argued, not unreasonably, that having thrown off the domination of one leader, King George III, it made no sense for Americans to submit themselves to another leader.

However, George Washington and his allies argued that the newly independent American states were vulnerable to both internal disorder and rebellion and foreign interference and invasion. Isolated and alone, the states would struggle to survive, but centralised leadership would bring them together and make them stronger. Ultimately Washington and his friends won the day and in 1789, six years later, he was elected president. Even then he faced several rebellions by people who challenged his authority.

Leadership can unite people around a common cause and make them stronger. Some of the other claimed benefits of leadership are:

1. *Creation and dissemination of inspiration and purpose.* Leaders like Washington bring people together by reminding them of their shared values and what unites them. In an article entitled 'What Leaders Do', leadership scholar John Kotter gives the example of Lou Gerstner, CEO at American Express, who challenged established beliefs at the company and helped it to rediscover its purpose and give it a new direction. Kotter also talks about the role played by leaders in aligning people with purpose, in order to make sure that everyone is pulling in the same direction, by first defining what the purpose is and then communicating that purpose through the rest of the organisation.
2. *Motivation of others.* By reminding people of the purpose, leaders also remind their followers of why they came together in the first place. This reminder of purpose helps people to discover – or rediscover – meaning in their work, and has been shown by many decades of research to be closely linked to higher performance and better organisational outcomes, as well has having positive psychological effects on the people themselves.

3. *Provision of skills and knowledge.* The group as a whole may lack certain vital skills that are needed to perform tasks and reach goals. A leader can help provide direction and coordination, and also share skills so as to benefit the entire group. Coaches and managers of sports teams and individual athletes are a good example of this. They draw on their own wisdom and experience to develop tactics and systems that will enable their followers to succeed.
4. *Resource provision and protection.* Even skilled teams and groups need resources – money, technology, training and practice, time – in order to reach their goals. Leaders who have access to resources and can unlock them for the organisation's use are a valuable asset to the organisation itself. Good leaders also protect their teams and organisations and give them the freedom to do their work without interference. A former colleague in Mumbai once described himself as an umbrella, shielding and covering his followers and keeping them safe from whatever was falling on them from above.
5. *Developing other people.* Leaders can help other people in their organisations to develop their own skills, knowledge and confidence. In effect leaders act as mentors for their people, encouraging them to learn, giving them permission to experiment and take risks, and generally helping them to fulfil their own personal ambitions. This too has been shown to produce better outcomes both in terms of organisational performance and human happiness. Most of us want to become better at what we do and who we are, and good leadership can help us to do that.

Two points need to be made in closing. The first is that these are *claimed* benefits; they do not always materialise. Sometimes, indeed, we see the opposite: no clarity of purpose, demotivated and poorly skilled people, oppressive deadlines set with no resources provided to meet them, bullying and coercive control that does harm to people within organisation. Good leadership will provide benefits to other people, but good leadership is not always present.

The second point concerns over-reliance on leaders. We are all capable of motivating, inspiring and developing ourselves, and we also have the capacity to seek knowledge and resources for ourselves: indeed, we do all of these things in our daily lives. Leaders can help us to go further than we might be able to go on our own, but ultimately we all have to take responsibility for our own lives. Otherwise, there is a risk that Thomas Jefferson was right, and we cease to be 'free and moral agents'.

WHO LEADERS ARE

In the section on misconceptions about leadership, above, we made the point that leaders are not just found at the tops of organisations. They are everywhere. In businesses we have team leaders, supervisors, office managers, heads of functions, heads of departments or divisions and so on, all of whom have leadership responsibilities. Military units have strong hierarchies of leadership defined by ranks a person holds, but some armed forces give leadership training to everyone, even the most junior soldiers, sailors or aviators, on the grounds that in a crisis anyone could find themselves in a position where they need to lead others.

We made the point too that leadership does not depend solely on legitimate authority. We might look to others for leadership because they have a particular skill or have important knowledge or background experience that will be useful to us, and we look to these people to show us what to do. Often this leadership is *situational* and *emergent*: depending on the circumstances we are in, we will look for a specific kind of leadership. People who we had not really thought of as leaders will step forward and take charge. We saw this in many settings during the Covid-19 pandemic, when the legitimate leaders had no idea of how to respond to the situation but other people – sometimes quite junior team members – stepped in and filled the gap.

Thus far we have made a distinction between leaders and their followers, the people who accept leadership from another person and follow their direction. In reality, though, all leaders are also followers. Team leaders lead their teams, but they are also followers of their department heads, who are in turn followers of the executive directors. Even the chief executive of a business is nominally a follower who reports to the board of directors; and also, as the political thinker and leadership writer Mary Parker Follett noted back in the 1920s, the topmost leaders of an organisation are also required to follow the organisation's purpose and mission. So, a senior religious figure like the Archbishop of Canterbury or the Dalai Lama is also a follower in the sense that they must uphold the values of their faith.

When we talk about leadership, therefore, we need to remember that leadership doesn't just involve the chief executive, the prime minister, the general or the chief constable. It includes all of the other leaders as well, right down to the lowest level, even including ourselves. If we are in a position of responsibility for the work of other people, no matter how many or how junior, then we can be defined as leaders. And further, distributed leadership means that leaders are also followers. The people we lead look to us for the leadership *they* need, and we in turn look to others for the leadership *we* need. This happens in every organisation, everywhere, all the time.

To sum up, it can be quite difficult to tell who is a leader and who is a follower. Many studies of leadership concentrate on top leadership: generals, prime ministers, chief executives and so on. But these leaders are really only the very small tip of a very large iceberg. They are also probably not representative of how leadership is experienced by others in the organisation. For most of us, the chief executive and the prime minister are remote and far away. The leaders who really impact on us are our own immediate bosses at work, and the local councillors in our own towns and villages and neighbourhoods; and what is more, the challenges faced by those local, immediate leaders are probably quite different to those faced by the faraway leaders at the top of the pyramid. The problems they have to solve and the resources they are given to solve them will be of a different order of magnitude.

CONTEXTUALISING LEADERSHIP

As this book will discuss, there are principles of leadership which have universal or near-universal application: for example, the need to build trust with followers. In practice, though, these principles have to be contextualised depending on time and place. This brings us to the *when* and *where* of leadership.

Heraclitus of Ephesos, who lived around 500 BC, once said that 'no one ever steps in the same river twice, for it is not the same river and they are not the same people.' Although this sounds like a T-shirt slogan, Heraclitus was making an important point. Organisations and people both change over time, and the leadership they need will change too as they gain (or lose) confidence and knowledge. Younger people with lower levels of skill and experience might need more direct guidance and mentorship; older, more experienced team members are looking for clarity of purpose and resources to get the job done.

Leaders themselves also change over time. The experience of leadership, including successes and failures, will provide new experiences and build (or damage) personal confidence. Promotion to higher levels of authority with greater responsibility is another important source of change. The changing requirements of leadership combine with the changes in leaders themselves to create a dynamic that means we are constantly adapting how we lead. Leadership is sometimes described as journey, and it is important to chart a course and know where we are on that journey.

In terms of place, culture is an important influence on leadership. Culture can be understood on several levels:

- National, regional and local culture including language and customs;
- Sector culture, the established customs and ways of doing things within a particular domain (banking, high-tech, charities, the military, government, etc);
- Organisation culture, the particular routines and habits of an individual organisation.

In some cultures there is an expectation that relations between leaders and followers will be formal and structured, while in others the atmosphere is more open and casual. Two identical organisations in the same sector might have very different cultures and views about what leadership is and how leaders should behave.

In leadership studies this notion that leadership always has to be contextualised is known as *situational leadership*. How we lead other people – how we gain their trust, to continue the example – will depend very much on time and place, who we are leading, where we are leading and when we are leading. What works in one culture or organisation might be a disastrous failure in another.

LEADERSHIP AS PROCESS AND SPACE

Treating leadership like an object or a thing that can be pulled apart or examined is to mistake the nature of leadership itself. Trait theory, which we will discuss in the next chapter, spends a lot of time trying to identify which characteristics and traits make for a successful leaders, but there is no evidence that *any* set of traits will guarantee success in leadership.

This is only the first chapter, but it should be already becoming clear that leadership is not a thing that resides in leaders, but an interaction between leaders and followers (who could of course also be leaders themselves). We need to think of leadership in terms of processes or activities – trust-building, relationship-building, motivating others, securing resources, identifying future needs, creating a compelling vision and so on – that are done in conjunction with other people.

These processes are not static things. They require energy to drive them, and that energy comes from both leaders and followers. Indeed, we could argue that one of the core tasks of leadership is to motivate other people and channel their energy towards the common goal. The coaches of a football team do not go out and score goals themselves. They motivate their players and show them how to use their energy to get results and win games.

Because of this, thinking about leadership is increasingly focusing less on the character of the leader and more on that interaction between leaders and followers. In their book *Exploring Leadership*, Richard Bolden and his colleagues conceptualised leadership as a 'space' inhabited by both leaders and followers. Leadership, they argued, was not inherent in a person, but in existed in the space between people. This concept of a *leadership space* allows us to see more clearly how the interactions work and how energy is generated and shared through the relationships we have with others. More recently, it has been argued that as well as leadership we should also be thinking about *teamship* and studying how teams are an integral part of leadership.

LEADERSHIP PARADOXES

Paradoxes are things that are evidently self-contradictory but are nonetheless a reality. They can take several forms. A famous example is the liar paradox. Take the following sentence: 'this statement is false'. Is the statement true, or is it false? It cannot be both at the same time. Another well-known example is the catch-22. In Joseph Heller's novel of the same title, a pilot tries to be declared insane in order to avoid being sent into combat. However, the desire to avoid fighting proves that he is a sane and rational person, and therefore he will not be declared insane.

Leadership is full of paradoxes. An example is the *paradox of I and we*. The leader is part of the team: they need the team to accomplish their purpose, and that means building strong relationships and generating trust with the rest of the team. At the same time, the leader is *not* part of the team: they must maintain a certain distance and separation. For example, there may come a time when the leader has to discipline a team member who is bullying or abusing others, or leaking confidential information. We can compare this to the dilemma faced by police officers when one of their friends commits a criminal offence, creating a contradiction between the need to preserve friendship and the need to uphold the law.

We will observe more of these paradoxes as we go through the book, but for now the main thing about paradoxes is they are not problems to be solved. We cannot break a paradox down and come up with a solution, as we might with a puzzle. Paradoxes are just there: they have to be lived with and negotiated. But, as we shall see, that is not always easy.

THE STRUCTURE OF THIS BOOK

The next chapter picks up some of the themes at the beginning of this one, and looks at how we think about leadership. From there, in Chapter 3 we dive deeper into the relationship between leaders and followers and look more closely at the leadership space, while Chapter 4 broadens out into leadership in larger and more complex organisations. Chapter 5 then deals with situational leadership and shows in much more detail how different cultures and contexts will influence leadership, enabling success and creating barriers at the same time.

Because leadership is situational and contextual, each leadership space will be different, and as we shall see in Chapter 6 this creates a problem for leaders: how do they project themselves into this space while still remaining true to themselves? How do they portray themselves as leaders while still being authentic?

Chapters 7 and 8 look at ethical issues. Leadership is full of ethical issues and dilemmas, and we will deal with some of these and show how ethics is vitally important to successful leadership. But we will also look at the darker side of leadership, a spectrum ranging from well-meaning incompetence to outright toxicity and even criminal behaviour by leaders. How do we avoid these things? How do we stop toxicity from spreading like a contagion through the organisation?

The final chapter, Chapter 9, looks at what leaders actually do in order to succeed. It may be tempting for readers to skip over the rest of the book and go straight to this chapter, but that is not advisable. In order to make leadership work in practice, we need to know the thinking behind it. Chapter 9 gives us the how of leadership, but we first need to be clear about the 5 Ws: the what, why, who, when and where. Chapters 2–9 will attempt to fill in these points.

FURTHER READING

Bolden, R., Hawkins, B., Gosling, J. and Taylor, S., *Exploring Leadership: Individual, Organizational, and Societal Perspectives*, Oxford University Press, 2011.

Chilson, N., *Getting Out of Control: Emergent Leadership in a Complex World*, New Degree Press, 2021.

Ferrazzi, K., *Never Lead Alone: 10 Shifts From Leadership to Teamship*, Harper Business, 2024.

Hersey, P., *The Situational Leader*, Prentice-Hall, 1986.

Kotter, J., 'What Leaders Really Do', *Harvard Business Review*, vol. 68, no. 3, 1990, pp. 103–111.

Witzel, M., Bolden, R. and Linacre, N., *Leadership Paradoxes*, Routledge, 2017.

2

HOW WE THINK ABOUT LEADERSHIP

Leadership is invisible and intangible. We can see and even measure its impacts on people, organisations and societies, but leadership itself has no physical existence. In turn, this means that we cannot pick it up, study it, examine it, dissect it, or subject it to scientific analysis with a view to forming firm conclusions. This is one of the reasons why studying leadership is actually quite difficult. We can observe what leaders say and do, but that doesn't necessarily get us any closer to what leadership *is*.

As leadership scholar Keith Grint points out, there are no agreed definitions of leadership. (Grint also asks an important question: does it really matter that there are no definitions?) Leadership is full of paradoxes – we'll be looking at a few of these in the course of this book – the first of which is that we can all agree that leadership is important but no one fully understands what it is. Look, for example, at some of the ways leadership has been defined:

- *Holder of the office of leader.* If I have a sign on my door that says BOSS, that makes me the boss.
- *The exercise of power and control over others.* The leader is the most powerful or the most dominant member of the community, the strong person who can enforce their will.
- *Defining and enacting values, purpose and mission.* Having done this, the leader then brings others to coalesce around this central core. Leadership scholar John Kotter argues that this is one of

DOI: 10.4324/9781003496243-2

the key attributes of leadership, one of the things that makes it a distinctly different activity.

- *Narration of purpose.* Similar to Kotter's view, this definition concentrates on leaders as explainers of purpose, as agents of change who will help people to understand why they should do what they must do. The leader sets the direction but also explains why that is the right direction.
- *Getting things done through other people, willingly.* This definition comes from British leadership writer John Adair, who emphasises the word *willingly.* This definition focuses strongly on the outcome; the purpose of leadership is to get a positive result by working with a team to achieve a defined goal. This definition is very popular in the armed forces, for example.
- *Enabling people to do what they could not do alone.* Here the leader is seen as a kind of facilitator who enables other people to reach a common purpose. People may wish to reach a desired goal, and the leader is the person, or people, who help them get there.
- *Development of other people.* 'The great leader can reveal new powers within me to myself', said the sociologist Mary Parker Follett. 'There is energy, passion, unawakened life in us – those who call it forth are our leaders.' Follett is arguing here that the primary task of leadership is to help other people understand and realise their potential, perhaps even by creating more leaders.
- *Different from management.* A great deal has been written about whether there is a distinction between leadership and management, with many authors arguing that management is more about process and function and leadership is about vision and mission. But there is a logical fallacy here. If we cannot define what leadership is, how do we know it is different from management? Even if we could prove that leadership and management are different things, and show how and why, the reality is that the same people are usually doing both.

Individually, none of these ideas comes close to explaining what leadership is. Taken all together, they *might* get us closer to a full definition of leadership, but all of these ideas also have a fatal flaw. None of them will actually work or have any impact unless people agree to accept them. I have a sign that says BOSS on my door, but if I give you an order and you refuse to obey it, my options are limited. I can threaten you, discipline you, even throw you out of the organisation, but you still won't have obeyed my order and my objective will not have been reached; and even if I *do* compel you to obey, I'll always be left wondering what will happen the next time I give an order. Similarly, I can talk until I am hoarse about the values and purpose, and I can try as hard as possible to help you develop and become the best person you can be, but if you refuse to listen or respond, I am wasting my effort.

The point is this: leadership is something that is done with other people. As leaders, we need the willing participation and commitment of others. So far as the definition of leadership goes, then, we need to recognise right from the beginning that leadership is a collective process. It is not inherent in one person; it exists in the relationships between people. So, instead of hunting fruitlessly for the one perfect definition of what leadership is, we need to recognise two salient points:

- Leadership is about other people, not just ourselves, and
- How leadership functions – how we lead, how others respond – will differ depending on the time, the place and the people themselves (in other words, leadership is situational).

WHERE DOES LEADERSHIP COME FROM?

Why are some people accepted as leaders? Why do others turn to them for leadership? Just as importantly, why do some leaders struggle to gain acceptance? Thinking about the answers to these questions is central to understanding what leadership is. Before we start looking at much more complex issues like why leadership is necessary (or is it?) and how to lead, we need to understand the origins of the concept. According to some anthropologists, our prehistoric ancestors lived in small family or clan units and may not have had leaders at all. Later, as more complex civilisations emerged, complete with features like cities, trade, agriculture and writing, leaders also emerged and took charge. But how did this happen? Where did these leaders come from?

The starting point for an understanding of leadership is this: in order for leaders to be accepted, they need to give other people reasons to follow them. Standing in front of people and declaring, 'I am your leader', is never going to be enough. Many have tried to do this, and failed. Put simply, followers need something to follow, some kind of inspiration or sense of purpose that matches their own needs and values.

Over the course of history, four sources of legitimate authority have been cited by leaders as reasons why other people should follow them: *'divine' right*, *inheritance*, the *consent* of followers, and finally the legitimate *devolution of power* from other leaders.

By *legitimate authority*, we mean the basis by which a leader holds a position of leadership, and which other people are required to recognise. Legitimate authority is not always – or even often – necessary for a leader to be successful, but understanding the sources of legitimate authority is a useful starting point.

'DIVINE' RIGHT

Leaders in early civilisations often tried to get around the problem by declaring themselves to be gods, hoping that if they could convince followers that they had divine powers they could compel obedience. The first person to try this was probably Naram-Sin, who ruled the empire of Akkad in modern-day Iraq from 2254–2218 BC, but there are other examples too: the *devarajas* or god-kings of the Khmer Empire in modern Cambodia after 800 AD, or Caligula, the third emperor of Rome, who declared himself to be a god in 40 AD and ordered a temple to be built so that people could worship him.

There is considerable doubt, however, as to how widely these claims of divinity were believed by followers. Many other Roman emperors were declared to be gods, and some ruled successfully. However, those who succeeded were also competent leaders who looked after their people. Those who were *not* competent often didn't last very long: Caligula was assassinated only a year after his proclamation of divine status. Naram-Sin faced a number of rebellions, and Khmer emperor Harshavarman II was overthrown and died in exile.

A less risky approach was to declare that the ruler and their family were descended from divine beings, or at least enjoyed the protection of the local deities. Examples of this are found around the world, in South America, Africa, Asia, Hawai'i and Europe. In ancient China a doctrine called the Mandate of Heaven was developed around 1120 BC which declared that the incumbent emperor was favoured by heaven, and must be obeyed absolutely; to challenge the monarch was equivalent to heresy. Much later in Europe we find another doctrine, the Divine Right of Kings (and Queens) attempting to establish the same principles. In both cases, these doctrines were promulgated with the hopes of warding off rebellions by fractious followers, by attempting to remove the legal and moral right to rebel.

How much real impact these doctrines had is debatable. Strong rulers enjoyed success, but there is a chicken-and-egg problem here: did people obey rulers like Louis XIV of France (reigned 1643–1715) because they believed he had divine backing, or because he was a powerful and charismatic individual? Certainly these doctrines did not stop rebellions. King Charles I of England's claim to have divine favour did not stop him from being overthrown and executed in 1649. Justinian II, emperor of Byzantium, also claimed to have been chosen by God but was deposed in 695. In this case the rebels cut off his nose rather than his head, on the grounds that his disfigurement would serve as a sign that God had withdrawn his favour. Justinian got around the problem by making a false nose out of solid gold, and thus equipped he returned to power ten years later. The gold nose didn't work for long, however, and a few years later Justinian was deposed for a second time.

INHERITANCE

Another method of gaining acceptance was for leadership to become a kind of private property, which could be passed down and inherited. The crown belonged to the ruler, who could hand it on to one of their children. The same thing happened in businesses, where the owners of capital handed it on to their children. This continues to happen to this day: the Ambani and Birla families in India, the Lees of South Korea (founders of Samsung) and the Busch family who owned and led the Anheuser-Busch brewing company in America from 1880–2008 are among the more famous examples, but millions of small businesses are passed on from one generation to the next.

The principle of inheritance was enshrined in law which made it harder to challenge, and by and large, so long as the leaders were reasonably competent, there was little opposition. However, the inheritance model has three important risks. The first is that the new leader who inherited from the old one will turn out *not* to be competent, in which case followers will often turn quickly against them; Richard Cromwell, who succeeded his father Oliver Cromwell as Lord Protector of England in 1658, lasted for just eight months before the army pushed him out of power and restored the Stuart monarchy. Second, the leader has no immediate heirs who can take control, in which case vested interests will usually compete to see who can take charge. And third, the heirs may start to fight among themselves, with destructive consequences. The television series *Succession* (2018–23), which showed the conflicts between the heirs of a business empire, was fictional but the scenario it describes is very real.

LEADERSHIP BY CONSENT

The third source of legitimate authority is the consent of those who are being led, i.e. the followers. Leaders can be formally voted into power by followers, as happens in democratic systems: voters choose their representatives, sports teams sometimes vote for their captains, the pope is chosen by the College of Cardinals and so on. In small groups, an unofficial leader will sometimes be recognised for their skills and experience, and other people will turn to them for example. There is no legal basis for this, but because everyone else agrees to accept an individual as a leader, there is an element of legitimacy.

Leaders who are chosen by consent are more likely to have genuine acceptance and be able to engage with followers, whereas 'divine' right and inheritance are more likely to result in mere compliance with the law: 'I accept you as my leader because I have to, but I don't agree with you and I don't really like you.' Consent, on the other hand, is more likely to be expressed as: 'I accept you because I want you to be my leader, because you have skills and experience that I do not have, and you value the same things that I do.'

Despite this – and this may come as a surprise – genuine leadership by the formal consent of followers is surprisingly rare. Most workplace teams don't choose their leaders; students don't choose their teachers, and soldiers don't choose their officers. In the latter case there have been experiments with democracy: some pirate crews in the seventeenth century chose their captains, and during the Russian Civil War of 1917–22, units in the Red Army were allowed to choose their own officers, although this practice was quickly abandoned when it became clear that officers were being chosen for their popularity rather than their competence. This is a weakness inherent in any democratic model of leadership: leaders are sometimes chosen, not because they will be good leaders, but because followers like them personally and/or think they can control them.

Another question also arises: which followers have the power to choose leaders? In ancient Athens, the birthplace of modern democracy, in practice women and slaves were excluded from voting and only a few hundred men possessed the right to vote and choose leaders for themselves and everyone else. Most democracies extended the franchise only to people who had wealth and property; in Britain, right up to the nineteenth century, the borough of New Romney returned two representatives to the House of Commons, but only eight people were qualified to vote (out of a population of over three thousand). Universal suffrage only came into being in the twentieth century, and there are still restrictions: for example, in most countries people under a certain age are not allowed to vote.

In businesses, a new CEO may be approved by the vote of the board of directors, typically no more than a dozen people in company with a hundred thousand employees or more. So, when we hear that a leader has been chosen by their followers, we are entitled to ask: which followers did the choosing? And what about the opinions of the rest?

DEVOLUTION OF POWER

The most common form of legitimacy is the devolution of power from other leaders. In the UK, for example, the king devolves power to the prime minister, who in turn distributes power to members of the cabinet. Overall power is vested in the national government at Westminster, which in turn gives power and leadership posts to the four devolved nations – England, Wales, Scotland and Northern Ireland – and within each country to a network of county councils, district councils and parish councils, each with their own leader.

In a business, the chief executive distributes power to the other executive directors, who in turn create division and department heads, team leaders and so on down the line. When people talk about 'leaders' they often mean the people at the top or centre of the organisation, but in reality every organisation is a network of leaders who have been chosen or appointed by someone in a position of authority over them.

THE PARADOX OF POWER

People in positions of leadership are granted a great deal of power, but they can only use that power by giving it away to other leaders. This only increases as leaders become more senior and more prominent: the more power they have, the more they must devolve that power in order to be effective.

ACCEPTANCE VS ENGAGEMENT

As we said earlier, though, legitimate authority will – usually – mean that the leader is accepted, however grudgingly. But *acceptance* is not enough. If leaders are going to get things done, they need to be able to *engage* with their followers, to attract their attention, get them to listen to what the leader has to say and, ultimately, to get them do what needs to be done in order to fulfil the organisation's mission. To do that, we need to understand why people engage with leaders and are ready to follow them. Over the course of time there have been various theories about this.

BELIEFS ABOUT HOW LEADERSHIP WORKS

The understanding of why people follow certain leaders – and don't follow others – has been a subject of perennial fascination. Here are a few theories of leadership that have developed over time. Think about each in turn and what, if anything, it tells you about both the nature of leadership itself, and how people have *perceived* leadership.

THE 'GREAT MAN' THEORY

The notion of the 'great *man*' as leader is an important reminder of how leadership was seen in the past (and still today in some places): a male-dominated sphere, where only men were seen as having the capacity for leadership. When Mary II became queen of England in 1689, she handed over virtually all her royal duties to her husband, who became King William III. In business, women who were widowed could become leaders in the absence of their husbands, but usually only until their (male) children were old enough to take over. When the Englishwoman Eleanor Coade set up her own business supplying building stone in London in 1769, she had to describe herself as 'Mrs Coade' to gain acceptance, although she was never actually married.

The term 'great man' was coined in the nineteenth century by Thomas Carlyle, who believed that 'the history of the world is but the biography of great men', but the concept goes back as far as the Italian statesman Niccolò Machiavelli in the sixteenth century. Machiavelli believed that some people had been chosen by fate or destiny to be leaders, but he also argued that successful leaders had intelligence and powers of perception beyond those of ordinary people. In other words, leadership was not for everyone; only the special few could become leaders.

'Great Man' theory, as it was developed in the late nineteenth and early twentieth centuries by philosophers such Friedrich Nietzsche and William James, argued that 'leaders are born, not made'. The idea is quite simple. There is a mysterious essence that we may refer to as *it*. Leaders are born with *it*, others are not. You either have *it*, or you don't. For those people who do have *it*, there is a responsibility to step up and be a leader to fulfil your destiny. If you don't have *it*, bad luck.

So, what is *it*? Looking at the biographies of 'Great Men', a few factors stand out:

- *Charisma*. 'Great Men' have the ability to command the attention of an audience. They are often gifted orators, but they also possess a physical presence that makes other people pay attention to them. They can connect with other people almost without effort, and through that connection inspire others to share their vision and follow their lead.
- *Intelligence and perception*. Great leaders are faced with many challenges, and their ability to overcome these depends in large part on superior intelligence and the ability to see things other people cannot see. Creative thinking and ingenuity are also part of this; great leaders change the rules of the game, or even the game itself.
- *The ability to ride their luck*. Along with this, great leaders are able to take advantage of fortune. Machiavelli believed that fifty per cent of human affairs are decided by luck. The test of a leader is their ability to recognise fortune and take advantage of it.
- *Unshakeable self-confidence*. 'Great Men' are fully aware that they are destined to be great. This means that they always believe they are right and rarely, if ever, question themselves or their beliefs. This enables them to keep pressing forward in the face of adversity.
- *Determination and ruthlessness*. Because they are convinced that they are right, great leaders will do whatever is necessary to overcome obstacles and claim victory. Great leaders have strong moral codes and a sense of honour, but they will break their own codes in order to what is necessary. Paradoxically, this ability to violate their own morality is seen as one of the things that makes them great.
- *Heroic failure*. Curiously, not all 'Great Men' succeed in the end, but that does not stop them from being 'great'. The emperor Napoleon I of France is an example of this. Napoleon's final defeat at the Battle of Waterloo only added to his reputation; the manner of his defeat somehow contributed to his 'greatness'.

THE PARADOX OF FAILURE

Leaders who fail are still considered to be heroes and examples to be emulated. The notion is that they somehow chose to 'fail heroically', like the hero of Lord Byron's epic poem *Manfred* who chose death rather than submitting to authority. At the end of the poem Manfred remarks, somewhat fatuously, that it is 'not so difficult to die.' This attitude is believed to show self-confidence and ruthlessness, both of which are great leader traits. So long as the leader exhibits these traits they are considered to be 'great' regardless of the outcome of their actions.

But how do you know if you do have *it*? According to 'Great Man' theory, the best way to be sure is to study the lives of other 'great men' from the past and compare their attributes to your own. If you see something of Julius Caesar, or Napoleon, or Martin Luther in yourself, then you might well have what it takes to be a 'Great Man.'

Apart from the rampant sexism which ignored the presence of many capable and powerful female leaders in every walk of life, 'Great Man' theory had other weaknesses too. First, it tended to foster cults of personality which accepted the 'greatness' of an individual with no critical scrutiny of their achievements. Second, and related to this, greatness is in the eye of the beholder. To many people in Britain, even today, Winston Churchill is regarded as 'great' because he led the defence of the country in the Second World War. In India, however, Churchill is associated with the Bengal famine of 1943 which brought death and hardship to millions. The uncritical acceptance of 'Great Men' led later generations of leaders to imitate the beliefs and behaviours of their past heroes, because it was felt that these things were part of 'greatness'.

'Great Man' theory has largely been discredited in the academic study of leadership, but the concept still survives in popular culture today. Senior business executives, populist politicians and top-level sportspeople and coaches are often looked to as examples of 'great' leadership, and the idea that leadership is inherent in individuals is still commonly found. To really understand what leadership is, though, we need a more nuanced approach.

TRAIT THEORY

Starting in the middle of the twentieth century, the emphasis in scholarship shifted away from personality and character and more towards the qualities that made leaders successful. Early research into trait theory, as the new school became known, focused largely on *distal traits*, which can be loosely defined as those traits associated with outward character and expression, including personal motivation and values, intelligence and perception, and charisma and personality, all of which are discussed in the 'Great Man' theory section. Later work has combined these distal traits with *proximal traits* which focus more on necessary skills and knowledge: examples include the ability to assess and form accurate judgements about other people, creative and problem-solving skills, communication skills and decision-making ability.

This research showed that the concept of leaders as 'born, not made' might not be entirely true. Skills are not necessarily inherent; they can be taught. Education also has the potential to influence the distal traits, including character. However, trait theory has also been severely criticised for looking in the wrong direction. Little evidence has been found to suggest that possessing one set of traits makes a leader more likely to be successful than another with a different set of traits. How leaders *behave towards others* seems to make more impact than who they are or what qualities they possess.

BEHAVIOURAL THEORY

Behavioural theory comes out of behavioural psychology, a branch of psychology first developed in the 1930s. Proponents of the behavioural approach argued that observing leader behaviour rather than analysing leadership traits gives us the best chance of understanding what leadership is. The American psychologist Kurt Lewin developed the notion of *leadership styles*, meaning how leaders express themselves and relate to their followers. Although these are called 'styles', Lewin's classifications of leadership more closely resemble philosophies or approaches, how leaders feel about leadership and the choices they make when enacting leadership. Lewin classified leadership into three approaches:

- *Authoritarian leadership.* The leader alone makes decisions and then demands that followers comply. Followers will be rewarded for success but there are penalties for failure.
- *Democratic leadership.* The leader practises collaborative decision making, involving other members of their team and feeding their views and experience into the decision-making process. Leader and team take collective responsibility for the outcome: as a leader, my success is your success.
- *Laissez-faire leadership.* The term laissez-faire, meaning 'let it be', is a term from economics and referred originally to the idea of letting markets take their natural course rather than regulating them. In leadership terms, laissez-faire means devolving decision making to the team and trusting them to come up with the right solutions. The leader only intervenes if needed.

Along with this comes another approach that categorises leadership behaviours according to function and outcome. Again, although these are called 'behaviours', they are also actions: we could think of them as behaviours translated into action.

- *Task-oriented behaviours.* These are behaviours/actions that focus on achieving goals: examples include delegating responsibilities, setting goals and targets, establishing the process for reaching those targets, measuring progress and solving problems.
- *People-oriented behaviours.* Included here are behaviours/actions that involve other people around the leader: providing support and encouragement, ensuring good communication, building trust and relationships, and ensuring that people are engaged with the leader and with each other.

The combination of these 'approaches' and 'actions' gives us something we could more clearly call a leadership style: what a leader imagines leadership to be, combined with how they then perform,

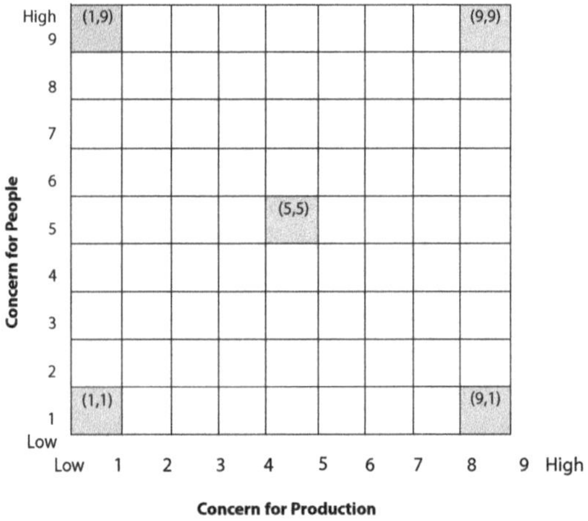

Figure 2.1 The leadership grid

Source: Adapted from Blake and Mouton, *The Managerial Grid III: The Key to Leadership Excellence*.

what they think and what they do. Two more scholars, Robert Blake and Jane Mouton, combined these factors into what they called the 'managerial grid' (somewhat controversially, they took leadership and management to be the same thing) and which we will call the 'leadership grid'.

The 'Concern for Production' axis is similar to the task-oriented approach we saw above, while the 'Concern for People' axis equates to people orientation. Each dimension is scored on a scale from one to nine representing how task-oriented or people-oriented the leader is. Blake and Mouton grouped the leadership styles on the grid into five classes:

- *Impoverished leadership (1, 1).* This is an ineffective form of leadership where the leader does not appear to be interested in much of anything. Followers receive few instructions and are given little direction; targets are set, but no one really knows how they are supposed to achieve them. This style combines elements of authoritarian and laissez-faire leadership; there is no sharing of control of power, but equally there is no direction. The leader might as well be invisible.

- *Task management (9, 1).* Sometimes known as 'produce or perish', this is a highly authoritarian style of leadership where the leader sets targets and issues instructions which others are expected to follow. Failure to reach targets can result in sanctions and punishment. The leaders sees followers as means to an end and has no interest in their development or satisfaction.
- *Middle of the road (5, 5).* This is laissez-faire leadership, where the leader sets goals and then lets followers pursue them however they think best. This can work very well if the followers believe in the same values and goals as the leader. However, where there is no alignment of goals and values, followers can sometimes drift away from the main objective, meaning a lot of effort and resources are lost.
- *Country club (1, 9).* In this style, the leader concentrates on setting the best possible environment and making sure people have the resources they need. We can see this as a combination of the democratic and laissez-faire approaches. The leader's chief purpose here is to make sure that everyone is happy and comfortable. The needs of the team are given priority over the goals of the organisation. Although this can result in happy and satisfied followers, there is an obvious risk that the goal will be neglected.
- *Team management (9, 9).* This is democratic management, where the leader's focus is on both people and task: how do we help people to achieve their task? There are similarities to servant leadership (see below). Team management is generally considered to be the 'best' kind of leadership in that it both satisfies and motivates followers on one hand, and achieves goals and missions on the other.

Behaviour theory is useful in that it helps us to understand more about the relationship between leaders and followers, but it has limitations. First, it ignores the relationship between personality and behaviour; how we behave towards others is conditioned in part by our own personal mindset and outlook on the world. Second, it does not take into account the situational element, and the notion that behaviours might have to change depending on what else is going on around us. The 'country club' style might work well if we have a skilled and experienced team, but if followers are less experienced or lack skills, a more interventionist style might be required. Finally, perceptions of the behaviour of others can be highly subjective. For example, two different observers plotting the behaviour of a leader on the Blake-Mouton grid might score that leader in very different ways, depending on how they interpret the behaviours they see.

THE PARADOX OF PERCEPTION

The interpretation of a leader's actions will always be subjective. One person observing a leader might take a positive view of that leader, depending on their own circumstances and the impact on themselves; another might take a negative view. Think for example of the restructuring of a team, where one member is promoted to a position of more responsibility and given a salary increase, while another is no longer necessary to the team and is transferred out or made redundant. Each will have different views of the leader, and each will be entirely justified in holding those views, despite the fact that they contradict each other. So, the leader is both 'good' and 'bad'.

CONTINGENCY THEORY AND SITUATIONAL LEADERSHIP

Building on behavioural theory, in the 1960s scholars including Fred Fiedler, Paul Hersey and Ken Blanchard began to develop more advanced theories that suggest that how effective leaders are depends on a combination of their own abilities and the situations in which they find themselves. Fiedler's *contingency theory of effectiveness* matched the concepts of task orientation and people orientation with three sets of situations:

- Favourable situations, which are well suited to a leader's orientation;
- Unfavourable situations, which are not suited to a leader's orientation;
- Intermediate situations, which are neither favourable nor unfavourable.

A leader who has a strong task orientation will struggle in a situation where the clear priority is to motivate people, to lift their spirits and inspire them to carry on with the job. Similarly, a leader with a strong people orientation may not be able to make impact when the main priority is to complete the task as quickly and efficiently as possible; they may spend too much time worrying about people's feelings when they need to be thinking about getting the job done.

All of this means that, once again, there is no right way or wrong way to lead people, but only the best way for that time and place. Leaders need to be prepared to adapt their style to circumstances. In peacetime, a military officer may need to adopt a people orientation, preparing their troops and ensuring they have the right skills and their morale is high, but in wartime the emphasis may shift to completing missions and achieving objectives.

This leads us to *situational leadership*, where Hersey and Blanchard built on contingency theory but also added another element, the abilities and skills of followers. Hersey and Blanchard defined four leadership styles:

- *Delegating*: characterised by weak task behaviour and weak relationship behaviour: the leader delegates authority to the group and monitors but does not participate.
- *Participating*: characterised by weak task behaviour and strong relationship behaviour: the leader is one of the team, working with them to reach decisions collectively and not imposing their own will on the group.
- *Selling*: characterised by strong task behaviour and strong relationship behaviour: leaders lead by persuasion, inspiring or encouraging their group to complete the task.
- *Telling*: characterised by strong task behaviour and weak relationship behaviour: a directorial style where the leader tells others what to do without encouraging input from followers.

Following from this, Hersey and Blanchard also define what they call the *performance readiness* of teams and groups in terms of how ready they are to complete a given task:

- *R4: able, confident and willing*: the team are both willing to carry out the task and confident that they have the skills to carry it out. They believe they will succeed.
- *R3: able, but insecure and unwilling*: the team probably have the skills and experience they need, but they either do not understand the task or do not believe that this is the right course of action. They have the abilities, but no faith in success.
- *R2: unable, but confident and willing*: the team know they have weaknesses; perhaps they are faced with the challenge of something they have never done before, or are in a competitive position where they know they face superior opposition. Despite the odds against them, they are willing to try.
- *R1: unable, insecure and unwilling*: the team are faced with an unknown situation, or know they lack the skills and experience to succeed. As a result, they have no belief that they will succeed, and will regard trying to complete task as doomed from the start.

Different leadership styles will be required depending on the state of performance readiness. A team in the R4 category, for example, might be best suited by a 'delegating' style: the team know what they need to do, so let them get on with it. A team in the R1 state might need a 'selling style', where the leader both helps them understand the task and acts as cheerleader, motivating them to believe in themselves. An R3 team might also benefit from a 'selling' style, but a 'participating' style might also be useful, where the leader mixes with the team and encourages them. With an R2 team there might be a place for the 'telling' style, where the leader acts as instructor and tutor.

The point is clear: leaders need to be able to adapt their approach to leadership depending on the situation in which they find themselves. We will look at situational leadership in much more detail later in this book.

TRANSACTIONAL VS TRANSFORMATIONAL LEADERSHIP

One of the most commonly found distinctions in leadership styles is between *transactional leadership* and *transformational* leadership, first popularised by James MacGregor Burns in 1978. Transactional leadership sees leadership as a bargain between leaders and followers, a process of exchange whereby each gets something that they want. Leaders provide direction, skills and reward; in return, they receive the productive outputs of followers which enable the leaders to meet their own goals. Put more simply, I as a leader provide you with work, give you instructions and pay you well; in exchange, you work hard and get the job done. Both of us are satisfied.

Transformational leadership, on the other hand, is where leaders influence followers – and vice versa – in order to help them achieve personal growth and transformation. Recall the quote from Mary Parker Follett, above: 'There is energy, passion, unawakened life in us – those who call it forth are our leaders.' Follett was writing in 1928, fifty years before Burns, but they are talking about exactly the same thing. Instead of seeing leadership as a bargain, transformational leadership imagines leadership as a process of influence and inspiration which benefits all parties.

Transformational leadership is usually seen as the 'better' style of leadership. It accords with motivation theory, which holds that people are more strongly motivated by personal satisfaction and opportunities for growth than they are by the chance of reward. There is a considerable body of evidence that suggests that this is indeed the case. A transformational approach will usually get more out of people than a purely transactional style.

However, there are weaknesses in this concept. Most importantly, transformational leadership ignores outcomes: what are we transforming people into? What are we motivating them to do? Transformative leadership can be used negatively as well as positively, and people can be influenced to harm others or commit crimes. It becomes important to have leaders with clear moral compasses and strong ethical mindsets.

THE PARADOX OF INTENTION

Having a moral compass is important, but again we need to ask a question: whose morality are we discussing? There is an old saying that 'one person's terrorist is another person's freedom fighter.'

Demonstrators in favour of proscribed organisations like Palestine Action believe that they are upholding human rights. Others see them as supporting terrorism. Depending on your standpoint, either position could be true.

SERVANT LEADERSHIP

'Servant leadership' may sound like an oxymoron, but the concept actually has ancient roots, stretching back to the notion of laissez-faire and from thence to Daoist philosophy in ancient China. Recall the quote from the *Daodejing* in the introduction: 'The highest type of leadership is that of which the people are barely aware.' In other words, leaders should trust followers to know what to do, and only interfere if things begin to go wrong. In the European Enlightenment of the eighteenth century, some rulers like King Frederick II of Prussia (Frederick the Great) began to neglect the notion of absolute monarchy, arguing that they were the servants of the state rather than its rulers.

In modern times the concept of servant leadership was first formulated by the business executive Robert Greenleaf, who came ultimately to the same conclusion as Frederick the Great: the leader of any organisation is ultimately the servant of that organisation and, by extension, the servant of the people in that organisation. We have to be careful here: 'servant' in this context does not mean 'servile' or inferior. Back in 1928, Mary Parker Follett had observed that both leaders and followers are ultimately followers together, serving what she called 'a higher purpose'. The purpose and mission of the organisation are the ultimate masters, and the leader is there to serve that purpose and mission.

This ultimately led to concepts like *stewardship*, where the leader is seen as holding responsibility for the whole organisation. Most organisations outlast their leaders, so one of the leader's tasks is to preserve and enhance the organisation and hand it on to their successors in a healthy condition. A second strand of servant leadership suggests that the job of the leader is to support followers and help them to progress and develop, along the lines of transformational leadership (above). As leaders, we should be guides, mentors and coaches to our followers, to enable them to develop to the same level as us. The first job of the leader, it is sometimes said, is to create and grow other leaders.

A metaphor sometimes used when discussing servant leadership is that of the shepherd, whose primary purpose is to guard their flock. In Mediterranean countries, shepherds do not lead their sheep or goats out to pasture; the animals already know the way. The shepherd follows behind, sweeping up any animals that might be get lost and setting them back on the correct path.

Again, there are limitations to the concept. As we saw in the discussion of situational leadership, some followers need more guidance than others. The shepherd can follow behind so long as the goats know the way to the pasture, but may have to take the lead when it comes time to switch to new grazing grounds. Sometimes, the servant may have skills and experience that the master does not, in which case they made need to change roles. In barracks, the soldiers report to the officer and obey their orders, but out on patrol, it is the scout who goes out in front of the platoon to survey the ground who takes charge and gives direction to their comrades. All of this means that 'service' is a malleable concept and servant leadership will take different forms depending on the situation.

LEADER-MEMBER EXCHANGE AND THE RELATIONSHIP SPACE

Another criticism of servant leadership is that it can feel a bit uni-directional. The leader serves followers, but what does the leader get in return? The concept of *leader-member exchange* seeks to redress this. Leaders and followers influence each other; leaders react to follower behaviours. Politicians will respond to changes in voter perceptions and beliefs, changing their own views or at least opening themselves up to ideas that they might previously have disagreed with. There is a common saying at the Royal Military College, the principal training ground for army officers in the UK: 'never give an order unless you know it will be obeyed.' In other words, good officers are in tune with their soldiers, know what they are capable of what they are willing to do. Leo Tolstoy observed this in his novel *War and Peace*, in an incident where junior officers were puzzled by the lack of orders from their general. The answer was simple, said Tolstoy: the general was waiting until the army knew what it wanted to do.

This notion of 'exchange' leads us to a very important point. Exchange is not a thing, it is a process; a transaction, if you like. Leadership is not something that leaders do *to* people; it is something they do *with* people. This is the point that Richard Bolden and his colleagues made in their book *Exploring Leadership* (see also Chapter 1). They explicitly defined leadership as a two-way process that links leaders and followers. The implication is that leadership is not something that inheres in people, but is to be found in the 'leadership space' that encompasses a group of people, some of whom we might identify as leaders and some of whom are regarded as followers. How they work together, how they behave towards each other, determines how leadership is enacted.

Another version of leader-member exchange can be found in the work of the British consultant and academic John Adair, who argued that leadership is a combination of three factors: the individual team member (which can include the leader themselves), the task and the team.

The important point about this diagram is that no one element is dominant. It is the combination of the three that makes up leadership. The leader has three responsibilities: to develop the team, to develop the individuals within the team, and to accomplish the task. But none of those three elements can be left out. Take away the team and there is just a collection of individuals; take out the individual element and the approach becomes directive and controlling; take away the task and all semblance of purpose disappears. The leader needs all three, and all three need the leader.

So, the answer to Keith Grint's question – does it really matter that there are no definitions? – is: probably not. We certainly don't need definitions of leadership as an object because it is not a *thing*; one cannot point to anything solid and concrete and say, 'there is leadership.' Leadership is a *process*. We can identify good leadership outcomes: happy people, prosperity, better healthcare outcomes, trophies won on the sporting field. We can also identify bad leadership outcomes: people who are made ill or are injured or killed

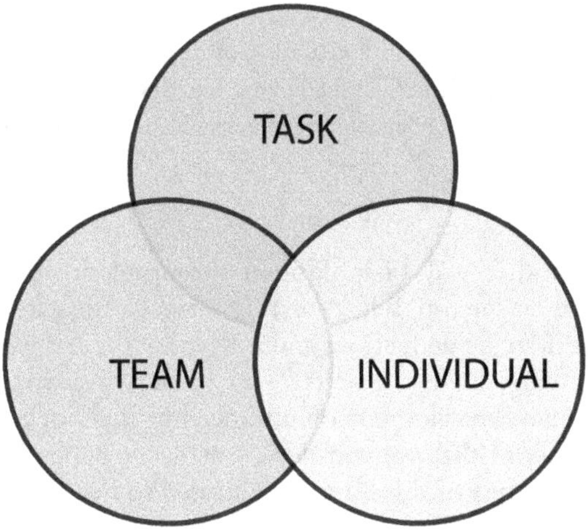

Figure 2.2 The three circles

Source: Adapted from Adair, *The Inspirational Leader: How to Motivate, Encourage and Achieve Success*.

as the result of leadership mistakes, for example. But we cannot see, tangibly, what led to those outcomes. The 'leadership space' is not demarcated by physical boundaries. It exists in the minds of leaders and followers, and only the outcomes of those processes are felt in the real world.

So, we need to stop thinking about leadership as a *thing*, and think about it instead as *space* and *process*, something people do with other people, in partnership with other people. And, because people are all different and have a myriad of different relationships with each other, the process of relationship is endlessly fluid; or, at least, it should be. If we try to put leadership into a box, define it, pin it down, there is a danger that we will lose much of that flexibility.

THE PARADOX OF MEANING AND DOING

We can never really know what leadership is, because it is constantly changing and shifting. At the same time, though, leadership is vitally important to the smooth functioning of organisations and society, so we need to get better at leadership and become more effective practitioners. But how can we be effective at doing something that we can't define?

There is another way of looking at the problem, however. We can't define leadership, but we can observe its impacts, and from those we can make deductions about what works and what doesn't work. We can also get a better idea of our own strengths and weaknesses and develop our own leadership style, or even better, a range of styles that we can deploy at need, depending on the situation. The rest of this book is dedicated to helping us do that.

SUMMARY

- Leadership is hard to define, but searching for precise definitions is probably a waste of time. There are other, more important questions to answer.
- The source of a leader's authority has been much discussed, but ultimately the only authority that matters is the consent of those being led, who agree to accept the leader.
- Leaders gain that acceptance by providing something that followers do not have, such as additional knowledge or skills.
- Leadership was formerly seen as a property or characteristic of individuals, but modern thinking focuses more on the relationship between leaders and followers.
- Situational leadership suggests that leadership will be enacted in different ways depending on the character of the leader, the needs of followers and the nature of the goal they are trying to achieve. Different leadership styles may be more successful in different situations.

FURTHER READING

Adair, J., *The Inspirational Leader: How to Motivate, Encourage and Achieve Success*, Kogan Page, 2005.

Blake, R. and Mouton, J., *The Managerial Grid III: The Key to Leadership Excellence*, Gulf Publishing, 1985.

Bolden, R., Hawkins, B., Gosling, J. and Taylor, S., *Exploring Leadership: Individual, Organizational, and Societal Perspectives*, Oxford University Press, 2011.

Burns, J.M., *Leadership*, HarperCollins, 1978, reprinted 2010.

Greenleaf, R.K., *Servant Leadership: A Journey into the Nature of Legitimate Power and Greatness*, Paulist Press, 2002.

Grint, K., *Leadership: A Very Short Introduction*, Oxford University Press, 2010.

Lewin, K., Lippitt, R. and White, R.K., 'Patterns of Aggressive Behavior in Experimentally Created "Social Climates", *Journal of Social Psychology*, vol. 10, no. 2, 1939, pp. 269–299.

Machiavelli, N., *The Prince*, trans. T. Parks, Penguin, 2011.

3

LEADERS AND FOLLOWERS IN TEAMS

It should be apparent by now that leaders only get things done through their followers. The leader-follower relationship is often an antagonistic one, with each side trying to dominate the other rather than working together to achieve a goal, but this becomes a fundamentally destructive relationship. Leaders and followers need to work together in order to reach their mutual goals.

The term 'followers' is controversial because it implies subordinacy: leaders set direction and the rest follow behind. But the relationship between leaders and followers is more complex than that, as we have already seen. In the example of the shepherd given in the previous chapter, the sheep and goats already know the way to the pasture, and the shepherd follows behind. We often talk about successful leaders or 'great' leaders, but their successes would have been impossible without the efforts of followers.

Leaders are sometimes influenced by a cognitive bias known as the Dunning-Kruger effect, also known as the myth of illusory superiority. Having achieved a position of power and authority, people allow themselves to be convinced that they are more intelligent, more capable and more highly skilled than others around them. Leaders are superior people, the thinking goes, so if I am a leader, it must follow that I am a superior person too; if not, I would never have become a leader. (This is of course a fallacy as there are many other factors – patronage, skill at political manoeuvring, luck – that could have contributed to a leader's rise to power.)

DOI: 10.4324/9781003496243-3

This bias tends to confirm to leaders that they are responsible for their own success and downplays the role of the followers.

The twentieth-century British businessman John Spedan Lewis was a victim of this bias. As he tells us in his autobiography, *Partnership for All*, he was convinced that the success of his department store chain (now the John Lewis Group) was down to his own qualities as a leader and strategic thinker. A serious accident left him unable to work for a long period of time, and he was at first convinced that the group would struggle without him. In reality the opposite happened: turnover, profits and customer numbers improved still further. Observing the continued growth of the business during his convalescence, Lewis realised that it was his employees, not himself, who were driving value creation. Until then he had thought of his employees as his subordinates, but now he came to think of them as partners. Returning to work, Lewis put this philosophy of partnership into practice by devolving ownership to his workforce, sharing knowledge with them and giving them a say in how the business was run.

The relationship between leaders and followers is often characterised by a contest for power, with each side trying to get control over the other. Leaders will also sometimes see output and reward as a zero-sum game. Workers should be rewarded only according to how much work they do, and each worker should get from their work exactly what they put into it, and no more. This leads to target-setting with rewards based on performance and, conversely, sanctions are imposed if the worker fails to meet those targets. These practices are widespread, but they are also damaging because they turn the workplace into an adversarial exchange.

Another business leader, Jamsetji Nusserwanji Tata, the founder of the Indian-based multinational the Tata Group, expressed sentiments similar to those of John Lewis. He too saw the relationship between employees and the business as a partnership. 'Our people are the sure and certain foundation of all our prosperity,' he wrote in the 1980s. He then went further still, stating that: 'what comes from the people goes back to the people, many times over.' In other words, said Tata, work is *not* a zero-sum game, and employees should receive far more in benefits than they contribute in productive labour. Tata saw work as a means of enriching people's lives and making them happy. (His workers rewarded this belief by contributing loyalty, high performance, innovation and quality that drove the business and laid the foundation for the Tata Group's future growth.)

We need therefore to spend some time thinking about the relationships between leaders and followers, what goes wrong and why, and some of the means by which we might get it right. Those relationships are of course contextual and dynamic: no one ever steps in the same river twice. In particular, there are vast differences between leadership in small groups and leadership in large, complex organisations. This chapter will be devoted to the first, leadership in groups and teams. In the next chapter, we will look at how we scale up and adapt some of these principles to leading teams of teams in much larger settings.

TEAMS AND INDIVIDUALS

There is a vast literature on teams, teaming, teamship and other related concepts. We won't go too deeply into it here, but we do need to understand a few principles of teams and team-working before we discuss leadership in teams.

The first and perhaps most obvious point to be made is that teams are composed of individuals. How well a team functions will depend on how well those individuals, who often are – and should be – from different backgrounds and had different life experiences, can work together. Sports teams provide a good example of this. It is sometimes assumed that putting the best players in a sport together will make the best team. In practice, though, all-star teams are usually beaten by more established teams who may be less talented individually but are used to working together.

THE PARADOX OF TEAM AND INDIVIDUAL

Team members work together and need something in common to unite them, but at the same time they need to preserve their individuality because that is what makes them valuable to the team. A team of people who are different but can work well together will usually outperform a team where everyone is the same.

The first challenge for leaders, then, is how to make these individuals work together as a team. In the past there was a tendency to enforce conformity: army units were taught to march in step, for example, to ensure that everyone did the same thing. Individual differences were ironed out or set aside. However, this approach to team-building is dangerous as it can lead to *groupthink*, where everyone agrees with everyone else and no one challenges the status quo, or *social loafing*, where some people will sit back and watch while others do most of the work.

There is of course no one-size-fits-all approach to leading teams because every team is different and the environments in which they operate are different as well, but we can observe a few elements that need to be considered by the leaders of teams. These are the *composition* of the team, the *processes* that enable the team to work, the internal *dynamics* of team relationships and the *values* that the team members have in common. All of these things are the concern of leadership.

TEAM COMPOSITION

Team members are individuals, but they shouldn't be just any individuals. In the workplace in particular, teams are often assembled randomly from whoever is available and/or willing. In the armed forces, too, people are often assigned to units or roles without any real concern for their aptitude or whether they can fit in. Getting the wrong people into teams can seriously hamper the efficiency of that team.

Team builders need to start by considering what the team's purpose is. Why does this team exist? What is it meant to do? Having firmly established the purpose, they should then think about what will be required of team members. What skills, knowledge and experience will be needed? How will the team work together? Can the work be divided into independent tasks where each can work separately, or will they need to pool knowledge and work as a unit?

Answering these questions will help shape the technical side of the team, who its members are and how they will work together, but we need to think about the social side as well. What is the team culture?

How is this impacting on the team's work? What could change to make that culture stronger?

Social identity theory, developed in the 1970s and 1980s, suggests that, among other things, when bringing people into groups we often tend to select people who share characteristics with us. They are part of the same 'in-group'. They may be of the same ethnicity or come from the same region, or they may have gone to the same schools and universities. Consciously or unconsciously, we perceive these people as familiar. We know we can get along with them. Inviting in people from an 'out-group', from a different background, is seen as more risky because we don't know these people or anything about them, and this leads us to think that there is a greater chance of conflict.

Two points are important here. First, conflict within a group is not necessarily a bad thing; indeed, if handled properly, it can be constructive (see below). Second, recruiting people who are too much alike can again lead to groupthink. Irving Janis, whose study of groupthink in governments remains one of the most important texts in the field, noted how groups who come from similar backgrounds often believed themselves to be superior at making decisions. In reality, they were quite bad at making decisions, in part because preserving group harmony took precedence over achieving the best result. Team members who disagreed with the rest of the group kept their doubts to themselves and went along with the majority in order to keep the peace, even though they knew the decisions the group was making were wrong and would have bad outcomes.

The psychologist Meredith Belbin also found that teams who came from similar backgrounds often failed. Sometimes, as Janis had pointed out, they failed to challenge each other enough, but Belbin found that in other cases they challenged too much. In particular, teams of highly intelligent people tended to get bogged down in arguments with each other as each member tried to prove their own superiority, and often took too long to reach decisions. Winning the argument became more important than reaching the goal.

THE PARADOX OF HARMONY (1)

Recruiting people who are similar to each other does not create harmony. Either people argue with each other to establish dominance, or they keep their doubts and reservations to themselves. In the latter case, as over the course of time it proves their doubts were well-founded, they grow resentful because they were not listened to (even though they could have spoken up but chose not to). Inviting in difference is more likely to lead to an effective group that works well together.

A final point about teams is that a good team usually needs a mixture of specialist experts and all-rounders. The specialists provide deep knowledge, while the all-rounders can move across different domains of knowledge and help to interpret what the experts are saying. Too many experts and the team may end up talking at cross-purposes, or the domain of knowledge may be too narrow to understand the problem and assess risks; too many all-rounders and there might not be enough deep knowledge to solve problems.

Recruitment should aim to meet the team's needs collectively, not individually; or in other words, each member should be able to contribute a piece of what the team needs, but they don't have to be good at everything. A sports team will have specialist forwards, defenders, goalkeepers and so on. Each is good at what they do individually, and leadership bring them together so they contribute their skills to the team.

The recruitment challenge for leadership can be summed up as follows:

1. Determine the purpose of the team.
2. Determine what the team requires to meet its goals.
3. Recruit a diverse range of people who can, collectively, fulfil those requirements.

TEAM PROCESSES

Teams work together by pooling their skills and resources to produce an output. Their work might be predominantly physical – laying a pipeline, erecting a building, assembling a car – or largely mental – designing a new piece of software, building a website – or some combination of the two, but either way they need to work together effectively. To do so, they need to share a common view about how tasks should be carried out.

Each member of the team needs to know exactly what their own role is, but they also need to know what others around them are doing so they can coordinate their efforts. Ivan Steiner's work in 1972 showed how failure to coordinate leads to what he called 'process loss', inefficiencies that arise when people aren't sure what they or their colleagues are meant to do. The most important team process is communication, which allows team members to synchronise their work, share knowledge and skills and solve problems.

From a leadership perspective, there are two ways of approaching team processes. Leaders could simply tell their teams what processes they use and how they will communicate, and leave it at that. Team members do the jobs assigned to them, knowing that if they fail to perform as expected they will be punished. However, there is a high risk that team members won't fully understand what is expected of them, which will lead to coordination issues, inefficiencies and process loss.

The other option is to explain the purpose and objectives the team needs to meet and then involve them in setting up the processes and designing communications channels. Highly skilled teams will do most of the work, or even all of it, meaning that the leader's task is to monitor and offer support where needed, rather than getting directly involved. Research shows that when teams design their own ways of working together, team members are more likely to understand what is required and are more committed to getting a result.

TEAM COHESION

The psychologist Bruce Tuckman suggested that teams go through four stages:

1. Forming: the group comes together and shares knowledge and understanding of the tasks they need to carry out.
2. Storming: the team learns to work together and builds trust, a process that could involve challenge and disagreement.
3. Norming: the team establishes its methods of working together and becomes a cohesive group.
4. Performing: the team works to achieve its goals.

Other scholars have added further phases including 'adjourning', where the team reaches its goals and then disbands, or 'reforming'.

The Tuckman model is still widely used, but it has also been criticised. First, the model assumes that all team members develop at the same rate and that team membership remains largely unchanged. In reality, team composition fluctuates. New members who join a team will still be in the forming and norming stages while longer-serving members will already be performing.

Second, the model also suggests that the 'storming' stage is where disagreements are ironed out and everyone agrees on the key points, leading to group cohesion. Thereafter, the group functions as a harmonious whole. Much has been written about the importance of cohesion and harmony in groups, but as Alasdair White points out in his book *From Comfort Zone to Performance Management*, too much harmony can lead to the creation of a 'comfort zone' where teams lapse into settled routines and fail to innovate or keep up with changes going on around them. High-performing teams are often ones that face challenge and stress, which spur them towards greater efforts.

Rather than everyone agreeing on everything and lapsing into groupthink, team members should feel able to challenge each other respectfully and in a professional manner. Discussing different ideas and alternative views is crucial to good decision making. Arguments between team member are not necessarily a sign that the group is falling apart; it may mean that the team members are exploring different alternatives and critiquing each other as a part of problem solving.

THE PARADOX OF HARMONY (2)

Teams need to work together, but disagreement and challenge are part of the process. Debate and harmony are both necessary for successful team working.

So, should leaders therefore encourage debate and disagreement? The answer in some cases is, yes. If team members are reluctant to challenge each other, the leader can step in and offer that necessary element of challenge. Alfred Sloan, the chief executive who made General Motors the largest company in the world, often did this with his board members. On one occasion, he asked the board if everyone agreed with a strategy that had been proposed. All of the other board members nodded yes. 'Very well', said Sloan. 'I am postponing discussion of the issue until the next board meeting. In the interim, please think of some reasons to disagree so we can have a proper discussion.'

TEAM VALUES

Argument and disagreement are effective so long as the team shares the same values and knows what its purpose is. We can have 'constructive disagreements' about how to achieve our goals, so long as we are fully agreed about what those goals are and why we are here.

Ensuring *alignment*, so that team members have the same values and clarity of purpose, is one of the tasks of leadership. Alignment should ideally be part of the recruitment process; teams should only recruit members who share similar sets of values. For example, a team with a strong focus on ethical behaviour and high professional standards might struggle to assimilate a team member who believes in success at any cost and that the ends justify the means.

However, the focus on values and purpose does not end there. Teams face a lot pressures: the need to contain costs, lack of resources, the need to hit deadlines, the loss of key members at critical moments, coordination challenges with other teams and many others. These pressures can easily distract team members from their purpose and erode the values. Leaders often talk about the need to constantly remind people of what they are trying to achieve and why. Some organisations put up posters in the workplace listing the organisation's values and reminding people of their responsibilities; others use informal group conversations and one-to-one meetings, allowing group members to give their own views on thoughts on values and purpose. These reminders are important to ensure that people remain motivated and focused.

WHY TEAMS WORK, OR DON'T WORK

From the above we can see that teams work well when the following happens:

- The right mix of people have been selected who have the skills to do what is required, with a diversity of background experiences to aid problem solving;
- All team members understand a) the purpose of the whole team, b) their own role in the team, what is expected of them and why, and c) what roles the other team members play and how to coordinate with them;
- The internal culture of the team encourages debate and challenge within respectful limits;
- Regardless of their other views, team members share common values and a sense of purpose.

Conversely, teams work less well when:

- People have been recruited into the team who lack skills and experience;
- Team members are afraid to speak up when they feel something is wrong, preferring to keep silent and not rock the boat;
- Team members are not clear about what they are meant to do, or why they are meant to do it;
- There is no common sense of purpose, which leaves people still more confused about what they are supposed to be doing.

These are not the only requirements, of course. Other issues such as lack of resources or failures of coordination at a higher level will also hold back performance. But in terms of the internal dynamics of the team, these are the things that will concern leadership the most.

TEAMS AND LEADERS

The following exercise, which is used for training purposes by emergency services in several parts of the world, illustrates how leaders and teams are interdependent.

THE BUCKET IN THE ROOM

A team is assembled, typically from eight to twelve people, with the objective of preventing a disaster. The team are asked to choose one of their number to be the leader. The leader is then taken separately to view the scene, a large open room with a bucket sitting on the floor in the middle. The bucket is (for the purposes of the exercise) full of a highly toxic substance. If anyone touches the bucket, or comes within three feet of the bucket, they will die. Furthermore, unless the bucket is removed from the room, the toxic substance will leak out and cause a major disaster.

The leader then returns to the team and explains the situation. The team are given five minutes to come up with a plan to remove using a few pieces of apparatus, usually a chair, a ladder and a length of rope, which have been provided. At the end of this time, the leader is told to leave: they are considered to be dead, and may not communicate with the rest of the team for the duration of the exercise. The rest of the team are shown into the room with the bucket so that they can carry out the plan.

The purpose of the exercise is to test several things:

- How well did the leader communicate the situation to the rest of the team?

- How well did the team understand what the leader was saying?
- How well did leader and team work together to make a plan?
- Did the leader ensure that the whole team understood the plan and everyone knew their part?

The leader needs the team because, alone, he will not be able to remove the bucket from the room. The team needs the leader, partly to give them the brief about what needs to be done, but mostly to ensure that the team members coordinate and understand the plan and what they need to do. Highly experienced teams will be able to work out a plan for themselves, but there is still a need to check and monitor that everyone is clear. With less experienced groups, the leader will need to coach and guide the members more directly.

When teams fail the exercise, it is because one of the four points above has not been fully addressed. The leader failed to fully explain the problem the team has to solve; or, the team misinterpreted what the leader was saying; or, the leader and team were working at cross-purposes; or, the leader failed to check with each team member to see that they knew what was expected of them; or, more likely some combination of most or all of the above. The point is this: leaders and teams need each other and have to work together.

WHAT TEAM MEMBERS WANT

People join teams in order to do something they cannot or would rather not do alone, to work, to protect and defend others, to engage in work or to play sports. Whatever they do, they are looking for the following:

- *Purpose and meaning in what they do.* In the workplace, research going back for nearly a century tells us that people want to know that their work is important and delivers products and services that other people need. Soldiers and sailors fight for their country and for freedom. Playing sports gives us a sense of well-being and we also enjoy the company of others. At work, at worship or at play, we seek fulfilment.
- *Reward.* We go to work to earn money, we play sports to win trophies or prizes, but there are other forms of possible reward

and gratification. Thanks and public recognition can be very important forms of reward that boost our self-esteem.

- *Personal development.* Joining different kinds of teams gives us the opportunity to grow in many ways: learning new skills, developing more confidence, improving physical health and well-being, and so on. Indeed, one of the benefits of working in a team can be improving our own ability to lead others.
- *Confidence and security.* While seeking fulfilment and reward, team members also want to know that they will be safe within reasonable bounds. Some occupations and sports are of course inherently more risky than others, but people will want to be sure that those risks are adequately controlled: workplaces are clean and healthy, machinery is adequately maintained and so on.
- *Control and freedom.* With some exceptions, team members want to be able to work or play in their own way, believing that they know best what needs to be done. The exceptions generally concern younger team members who lack experience and skills, or other team members undertaking a new task for the first time, who will want guidance and training. Otherwise, the last thing most team members want is micromanagement, people looking over their shoulders or constantly telling them what to do.

Whether team members get these things will strongly influence motivation and performance. If they find their work rewarding and fulfilling, are learning new skills and are able to work safely and free from interference, they are more likely to work hard and be productive. If any of these elements are missing, performance will start to fall away. For example, people might be working in a safe place with management that allows them a great deal of freedom, but if they don't find their work meaningful or rewarding, or feel stuck in a rut so far as personal development is concerned, their motivation will weaken.

WHAT LEADERS WANT

Leaders need teams to get the job done. They too want personal satisfaction and self-esteem, but success is also the basis on which they are also recognised and rewarded by their own leaders. Rightly or wrongly, assessments of a *leader*'s performance is usually based on how well their *teams* have performed. These are some of the things that leaders need from teams:

- *Willingness to work towards the common purpose.* Quite simply, leaders need their teams to commit to the job at hand. Forcing unwilling workers to complete a task is hard and there is no certainty that the job will be done well, or at all.
- *Time.* It may sound obvious, but being part of a team means the commitment of a certain amount of time, both for the work itself and for training and practice. How much time depends of course on the nature of the task at hand, and there are debates about how much time is required to be productive; for example, working shorter hours make team members more productive because they are less fatigued and get more done? Leaders need to calculate how much time team members will need to give.
- *Knowledge and skills.* Leaders are not the sole fount of wisdom in a team. Other team members will have experience and skills that the leader does not have, and leaders are reliant on those team members to complete tasks and reach goals.
- *Willingness to work with others.* Crucially, leaders need team members to be willing to work with each other to solve problems and complete tasks. Working together and thinking together creates *team cognition*, collaborative mental processes that form a kind of collective intellect that will be much more effective at problem solving than team members working on their own.
- *Reassurance and control.* Because the leader's own performance is based on the team's performance, leaders need reassurance that work is going according to plan and goals are being met. Sometimes leaders will set performance targets, known as *key performance indicators*, and ask their teams to report progress towards those targets. In other cases softer measures will be used, including one-to-one discussions or informal conversations with team members. All of these can help reassure leaders that work is under control and the team will be successful.

Control is a concept that can be interpreted in different ways. Some leaders think that control means the exercise of authority: if I give an order, my team members must obey it. That is a dangerous assumption. Whether team members really will obey depends on the balance of power between themselves and the leaders, and if the followers feel powerful enough, they may try to push back. They might do the bare minimum necessary to obey the order, they might leave the team in anger or in protest, or they might even feel bold enough to stay put and disobey the order. In the armed forces, authoritarian control was formerly the primary means of establishing discipline, but bad orders and incompetent officers often provoked mutiny. In France in 1917, the combination of an unpopular commander and a disastrous defeat led elements of forty-nine infantry divisions, about a third of the French army, to refuse orders from their officers.

The *leadership space* that we discussed in the previous chapter can be a contested space. If relations between leaders and followers become adversarial, the leadership space is the setting for a struggle for power. As Niccolò Machiavelli wrote in *The Discourses on Livy* back in the sixteenth century, 'if we consider the objects of the nobles and the people, we must see that the first have a great desire to dominate, while the latter have only the desire not to be dominated, and consequently a greater desire to live in the enjoyment of liberty.' Leaders want to control their followers in order to protect their own interests, while followers want to strengthen their own power so as to avoid being controlled. If a leader is perceived as being weak or lacking in power, followers might even try to throw them out and take control of the organisation themselves. This is what leads to revolutions and coups d'état.

Even if the leader wins the power struggle, a great deal of energy gets burned up and the organisation itself can end up weaker than before. Another approach, as already discussed, is for leaders to share power with followers. Giving followers more power – empowering them, in other words – will give them more freedom and control and reduce the likelihood of a power struggle taking place. Of course, if the leader gives away too much power, they risk making themselves redundant. The question for team leaders is, how much freedom can we give team members, and how much control do we need to keep for ourselves?

The answer will often depend on the situation. Again, younger or inexperienced team members may want more guidance and direction: empowering them and letting them get on with the job unsupervised could result in them becoming confused and fearful. Older, more highly skilled people may want more empowerment. As Rob Goffee and Gareth Jones wrote in their book *Clever*, leading clever people is more about creating conditions where they can work smoothly, giving them resources and protecting them from outside interference, rather than guidance and supervision.

Conventional wisdom suggests that when things are going well the leader can step back, leaving the team to get on with their work. When a crisis happens, that is when the leader needs to step in and take charge, and everyone else needs to follow the leader's guidance. However, this presupposes that the leader has all the skills and experience necessary to solve problems and lead through the crisis. In fact, as we saw when the Covid-19 pandemic broke out, people in positions of leadership were often powerless because they lacked those skills and experience, and it was left to others in their teams to step up and take charge. It is arguable that a time of crisis is exactly when the leader should rely on their team, like in the emergency services exercise given above. The question the leader needs to ask is not, 'how will *I* solve this problem?' but rather, 'how will *we* solve this problem?'

BUILDING TRUST IN TEAMS

The relationship between leaders and followers, the leadership space, is defined by a *psychological contract*. In some situations, such as work, we will have a formal technical contract that defines obligations and expectations on both sides. A contract of employment will specify what we are meant to do – with penalties if we fail to discharge our duties – who we report to, what financial reward we will receive and so on.

However, every organisation also has a psychological contract (sometimes also known as a social contract) with its members. Psychological contracts are often unwritten and unspoken, but they are an inherent part of any organisation's culture. They cover the things discussed in the previous section: what the team members expect from their leadership, and what leaders expect from their teams.

Trust is created in teams when the psychological contract is honoured by both sides. Both get what they want, which leads them to form a favourable opinion of the other side. Conversely, if one side fails to support the contract, the other side will lose trust in the relationship.

BUILDING TRUST

242 Squadron was a Royal Air Force fighter squadron sent to France in May 1940 to fight against Germany. The campaign was a disaster and the pilots of 242 Squadron took losses and only just escaped back to Britain, leaving their support crews and personal effects behind. They felt let down by their leaders, who had failed to properly support them and exposed them to high levels of risk. Some of their friends were dead. The pilots were demoralised and demotivated, and showed no respect to their superior officers. Their mood was not improved when they were informed that a new commanding officer had been appointed, Squadron Leader Douglas Bader, who had lost both legs in a flying accident some years earlier and had only just returned to active service. The pilots doubted whether Bader had the skill or experience to lead them into battle.

When Bader first joined the squadron, he realised at once that he would have to rebuild the pilots' broken trust. His first step was to climb into the cockpit of an aircraft and put on a dazzling display of aerobatics over the airfield, proving to the pilots that he was as good as they were. After landing, he called each pilot into his office and spoke to them one by one, asking what they needed. Many had only the clothes they were wearing and lacked essentials such as toothbrushes. Bader made sure that everything they needed was delivered the following day. There were also complaints about the food, so Bader fired the cook and brought in a new one.

Bader's actions showed the pilots that he could be trusted, and one half of the psychological contract was rebuilt. The second half came when the squadron was sent into the Battle of Britain. The pilots fought bravely and skilfully, thus proving to Bader that *he* could trust *them*. In this case the bond between leader and followers became very strong and 242 Squadron became an elite unit whose members trusted their leader and each other.

Trust is one of the bedrock elements of any team. When team members trust each other, they can achieve difficult things, even things that seemed impossible. Another example from the military concerns a case during the First World War when a party of Hungarian soldiers became lost in the eastern Alps during a snowstorm. Visibility in the blizzard was down to a few yards, and if the men remained where they were they would die of cold and hypothermia. No one knew what to do until one of the men found a map in his coat pocket. He persuaded the others that they could navigate their way out of the mountains, and the others put their trust in him and the map and followed his lead. Only after the men reached safety and were being given a hot meal did someone examine the map and realised it was of the Pyrenees, another mountain range hundreds of miles away. The map was irrelevant to their success; they escaped from the mountains because they trusted each other and worked together.

So, how do leaders build trust? The process takes time, and requires more than just words. Telling someone that they can trust you will not be enough to create trust (and in some circumstances it have the opposite effect, especially if people are already sceptical or suspicious. Here are some basic principles leaders should follow when attempting to build trust with their followers:

- *Make the other person feel valued*. When talking to other people, listen attentively and ask questions that show you have been listening. Make the other person feel like they are important. Learn about them as people. Find out what they need, what they are worried about, what their concerns are and make it clear that you are there to help them. Whatever their job or role in the team is, they matter to you.
- *Communicate your own values clearly*. Make sure that your team know who you are and what you stand for. Indicate clearly

any behaviours or actions by team members that will not be tolerated, but also show them what your own limits are. That way, when something happens or a crisis arrives, followers will know what to expect from you.

- *Be fair.* Leaders are sometimes required to be tough – when picking a team, for example, or making people redundant from jobs, or sending soldiers out to fight – but followers will usually tolerate toughness so long as the leader is also fair. It is important to remember that fairness and equality are not the same thing. For example, treating team members who are neurodiverse exactly the same as their colleagues will not result in fairness. True fairness lies in treating everyone according to their needs, in a manner that is consistent with justice.
- *Walk the walk.* Keep your promises. If you say you will provide something your team needs, make sure that you do provide it. That means of course that care must be taken when making promises: only make promises that you can keep. More generally, live your stated values and make sure your actions match your words. If you behave in ways that are not consistent with your values, followers will notice the discrepancy.
- *Show vulnerability.* Followers are more likely to relate to the leader and trust them if the latter is perceived as 'being human'. Admitting that you don't know the answer to a question, holding your hand up and apologising when you have made a mistake, asking forgiveness for being late to a meeting and so on are all examples of showing vulnerability in ways that will make followers more willing to trust you.
- *Ask 'why' questions.* When a team member behaves badly, breaks rules or fails at a task, don't simply punish them. Find out first why they have behaved badly and whether there are extenuating circumstances. Is the team member struggling at work? Are they having problems at home? When Squadron Leader Bader took over the ill-disciplined 242 Squadron, he did not punish his men for bad behaviour. Instead, he looked for the underlying problem and solved it, and as a result, the pilots began to trust him.

THE PARADOX OF WEAKNESS AND STRENGTH

Admitting weakness to followers can be a source of strength. Followers will perceive the leader as being fallible and vulnerable, just like themselves. This can create sympathy and loyalty in the minds of followers.

TRUST AND PSYCHOLOGICAL SAFETY

Much has been written about the importance of *psychological safety*, starting with the work of Carl Rogers in the 1950s and continuing with the more recent work of Amy Edmondson on links between psychological safety and learning. Essentially, psychological safety is a climate within teams where team members feel able to speak freely without fear of being punished or humiliated, either by the leader or by fellow team members. Research has shown a number of benefits from psychological safety, including the team's ability to learn from mistakes, a greater tolerance for risk when experimenting and trying new things, and opening up to learning and new information.

Psychological safety is only possible when team members trust the leader and trust each other. Both of these are essential. Admitting to a mistake, for example, becomes much more difficult if we believe there is a risk that our leader will punish us or our colleagues will point fingers at us and mock us for failing. As a result the mistake goes undiscovered, meaning that there could be risks of faulty systems, defective products, software defects that allow access to hackers or any number of other problems. On the other hand, if the failure is admitted, team cognition offers a chance to remedy the problem and learn lessons for the future. But this will only happen if the team members trust each other.

EMBEDDING DIVERSITY IN TEAMS

Trust is also critical when it comes to unlocking the benefits of diversity. We can think more narrowly of diversity in two ways.

One is to think of diversity in terms of categories such as those defined by diversity legislation: gender, ethnicity, religion, sexual orientation and so on. But diversity also encompasses broader categories such as different educational and socio-economic backgrounds, neurodiversity and different lived experiences. Even different career backgrounds can be a source of diversity: someone who has spent ten years working overseas will have different experiences and a different outlook on life from a person who has spent all of their working life in their own country.

Many organisations have initiatives to increase diversity of membership, but these initiatives have been subject to criticism. Some of this criticism is political in nature, but there are genuine risks associated with diversity. One problem lies in the difference between what organisations say about diversity and what they do: candidates from diverse backgrounds are brought in, but without psychological safety they suffer from prejudice and discrimination and are not able to be effective.

Another argument concerns tokenism: by introducing quotas for people from particular backgrounds, for example, organisations are effectively excluding other candidates who might have more merit. The emphasis, it is said, should be on diversity of thought and not diversity of background. However, the other side of the coin is that bringing people from diverse backgrounds is more likely to provide diversity of thought. A young woman from a South Asian background is likely to have a different worldview from a middle-aged white man.

On the other hand, many research studies show that diversity results in better decision making, including more effective problem solving and more thorough understanding of risks. Companies with diverse boards, for example, are more likely to recall defective products that might harm consumers. Diversity has real benefits and, for companies in particular there is good evidence that increasing diversity has a positive impact on profits and performance.

Simply bringing people from diverse backgrounds into teams is not sufficient. Social identity theory tells us that people tend to associate with people like themselves, forming 'in-groups' and 'out-groups'. The in-groups are people like us, whom we want to protect; the out-groups are the people who are not like us, whom we want (consciously or unconsciously) to exclude. Bringing in people from the out-group without any kind of preparation is risky. The two sides might not understand each other and refuse to work together. Factions might form and internal conflicts could break out, which will severely weaken the authority of leaders. Ordering people to understand each other and work together rarely works.

To repeat the point from the previous paragraph, preparation is needed. Before bringing in people from diverse backgrounds into the organisation, leaders need to be sure that the culture will be receptive. This means creating a form of psychological safety known as *inclusion*, where diverse people are made welcome and included in the in-group. Rather than focusing on the characteristics that make people appear to be different, leaders can emphasise the things people have in common: similar values, similar personal goals, similar ambitions and dreams. 'We may be different, but we are all here for the same reasons' is a good philosophy to cultivate.

KEY POINTS ABOUT DIVERSITY

- It must not be tokenistic. People will know when they have been appointed to a post to tick boxes or make up numbers. Many will find this offensive, as they are not being valued for their true qualities.
- Diverse people still have to be able to fit into a team. It is the leader's job to make sure that they can do so effectively.
- Communication and dialogue are needed so that people from diverse backgrounds can understand each other and assimilate new ideas.
- A culture of inclusion and psychological safety is essential to make diversity work.

In the words of the sociologist Vernā Myers: 'diversity is being invited to the party, but inclusion means being comfortable enough to get up and dance.' The leader here is the DJ, who chooses the tunes and creates the environment where everyone, regardless of who they are or where they come from, wants to dance.

UNLOCKING ENERGY IN TEAMS

In the previous chapter we talked about leadership as process rather than object. Trust-building is an example of a leadership process; generating psychological safety and inclusion is another.

Processes require energy to make them work, something that stirs otherwise static objects into action. Energy in organisations comes from two interdependent sources: leaders and their followers. Energy also comes in two forms: *impulsion*, which drives people to do things, and *direction*, which determines what things they choose to do. Both are necessary: impulsion without direction would mean that everyone did what they wanted without relation to anyone else, while direction without impulsion would just be an empty channel, like a dry riverbed when water has ceased to flow.

It would be tempting to say that leaders provide direction and followers provide impulsion, but it is not so simple as that. Traditionally, part of the job of the leader was to define the purpose and aims of the organisation, but these should not be simply imposed from above. Followers need to understand the direction and commit to it, a process often referred to as 'buying in'. If followers *want* to go in a certain direction they are much more likely to work hard to achieve goals, rather than merely following orders.

Earlier we cited the example from *War and Peace*, where the general waited until the army knew what it wanted to do. A personal anecdote from a business leader illustrates the point still further. On becoming a chief executive for the first time, this leader thought that it was her job to give directions which other people would carry out. She noticed, however, that her directions were not always followed, or were followed imperfectly with mistakes that had to be put right later and cost the company time and money. She realised that if, rather than giving directions, she asked questions – 'here is a problem, how are we going to solve it?' – her employees would think of the solution for themselves. Because they had been part of the process of direction-setting, they had 'bought in' and felt like they had a personal stake in the solution. Productivity and quality both quickly increased.

Impulsion brings us to the subject of motivation, which helps us to understand why people join teams and organisations, why they work and what they hope to achieve. Frederick Herzberg's classic work on motivation in 1968 divided motivational factors into two types: *intrinsic* factors such as achievement, recognition, desire to serve others, personal growth and ambition, and *environmental* factors, which he terms 'hygiene' factors, such as pay, working conditions, the quality of management and leadership, relationships with work colleagues and so on. Herzberg believed that intrinsic factors were the most important and long-lasting, but subsequent research suggests that environmental factors can play an important role too: we might be strongly motivated by a desire for personal growth and promotion, but if we are badly paid, work for bad managers and are surrounded by incompetent people, our motivation will soon begin to deteriorate.

Leaders can influence both kinds of motivation:

- *Intrinsic motivation*: leaders can ensure that there are opportunities for personal growth, promotion and fair reward. They can design jobs and tasks so that people find meaning in them and are able to see what value they are creating. Tactics such as *job enrichment*, aggregating sets of tasks into natural work units to make work more interesting and varied, can be complemented by innovative compensation schemes like profit-sharing or even employee ownership after the example of John Lewis.
- *Environmental factors*: leaders can set the conditions where work takes place. They can ensure fair remuneration and reward, safe workplaces, cultures of inclusion and psychological safety where people feel valued, and the provision of skills and resources required for success. Most of all, they can make sure that they themselves are effective leaders. Management quality is one of the most important environmental factors cited by Herzberg, the inference being that bad management and leadership are strong demotivators.

These are ways that leaders can contribute to the motivation of followers. Less commonly discussed is how followers motivate leaders. Interviews with senior leaders conducted over the years reveal how many leaders find that having enthusiastic followers who love their work and know how much value they are creating for other people is a strong motivating force for themselves. In the words of one leader I interviewed some years ago, 'The reason I get up and go to work in the morning is our people. They are just great at what they do, and they take immense pride in their work. It is a privilege to serve them.'

THREE LEVELS OF ENGAGEMENT

Ultimately, as leaders we need people to engage with us and the rest of the team to carry out the appointed task (think of the three circles model in the previous chapter). How strong that engagement is will have an impact on how well the team performs.

Engagement is usually described as having three levels. Different sources give different names for these levels, but the three we will use here are *compliance, internalisation* and *identification*. It should be noted that the boundaries between these three levels are porous and people will sometimes exist in a kind of partial state midway between two levels: think of this as a spectrum with three dimensions, rather than distinct states of being.

Compliance is the weakest level of engagement. People join a group or team because they feel they should, because of external factors like peer pressure, for example, rather than any strong internal motives. They pay lip service to the values of the group, but they don't really share those values; they may not even understand the values.

People comply with the demands of the leader and the rest of the group to avoid sanctions or being expelled, and they will expend the bare minimum of effort required to remain part of the group. Their loyalty is weak, and they might well leave the group at the first opportunity. Think of an employee who doesn't like their job, or someone joining a sports team who struggles to get along with their teammates.

It is usually easy to spot people who are 'dragging their feet' and not fully participating. As above, it is always worth asking why this is so. Why are they unhappy with their job, for example? Is it the work itself? Do they lack confidence, or skills, or resources? Do they not understand the purpose of their work, why they are doing what they are doing? If the leader knows the answer to these questions, they can provide remedies that might increase engagement.

Internalisation comes when we identify as members of a group and feel a sense of belonging, but still don't really understand values and purpose. We stay with the group because of the people; we like them, they are our friends and we feel loyal to them, but not to the overall organisation. This sense of unity might come from adversity, for example; people who feel they are experiencing bad leadership might band together to look after each other and push back against the leadership.

In these cases, the psychological contract might be strong with the rest of the team but weak or non-existent with leadership and outsiders. Again, it is worth asking why this is so. What is preventing wider engagement? The answers could include lack of understanding or knowledge about the overall purpose: I know what my team do, but I don't know what the rest of the organisation does. Strong in-group loyalties may be excluding out-groups, in which case the leaders need to break those barriers down. Finally, past bad experiences – weak or bullying leaders, broken promises, failures to provide resources and skills – may be causing people to withdraw into their shells. They feel they can rely on the other people around them, but no one else.

Identification is the strongest form of engagement, and comes about when people both fully understand the values of the group and feel that those values match their own. They join the group because they want to be part of the group, not only because of the other people in the group but also because of what the group itself represents. They might even refuse offers from other groups who offer them more tangible benefits because the first group is where they feel at home. In India, the Tata Group pays its managers less than some other business groups, but is still an employer of choice because of Tata's strong values and tradition of service to communities in India. Working for the Tata Group gives managers an opportunity to feel good about their work and about themselves, benefits that are more important to them than money.

Identification is what most organisations want because people who identify with the group are more loyal, work harder and are more creative and innovative. This time, the questions need to be flipped around: why do people identify? What is it about the organisation that inspires loyalty and commitment? For the Tata Group, it is that commitment to service to communities, the sense that the group operates for the benefit of the people rather than just to make money. For the John Lewis Group, share ownership gives employees a sense of participation; they are not just tools to be used by the company, they are part of it and help to determine its destiny.

REDESIGNING WORK AT RANDALLS

Randalls (not its real name) was a chain of small department stores operating across the UK, with a presence on most high streets. Lack of investment and a rigid structure led to demoralised and dispirited employees, poor quality goods and lack of customer service and, ultimately, declining revenues and profits that led the company to the brink of bankruptcy.

New owners rescued the company and sent in a new leadership team. The leaders found that the company was divided into 'silos', departments and teams dedicated to single functions where no one talked to anyone else. Each of the main operational elements of the business – procurement, distribution, store management, marketing, finance – existed in a silo, with little or no contact with the rest of the business. The mood was one of compliance: people turned up and did their jobs, but no one really cared.

The problem was particularly acute in the finance department. The only thing that most of the finance teams knew about the rest of the company was that everyone else hated the finance teams. Every time anyone proposed a new project that required money, the finance department refused the expenditure on the grounds that the 'rules' would not allow it. This was one of the reasons for the chronic lack of investment that was crippling the company.

The new leadership team responded by breaking down the functional barriers and abolishing functional departments. In their place, leaders created dozens of multi-functional teams, each focused around a particular product line. Each team contained representatives from all of the former functions: a single team would have specialists in all of the things above, procurement, distribution, store management, marketing, finance and so on.

The effect was transformational. The teams were now diverse, rather than all coming from the same background, and members contributed their own knowledge to help solve problems and innovate. Also, they could see the whole process from end to end, from buying in goods from manufacturers to the point of sale, and they could all get direct feedback from customers. Because they could now see what their jobs meant and the purpose of their tasks, their engagement increased dramatically. The finance members of each team now had a can-do attitude: if money was needed for investment, they could find it. Productivity increased, driving up sales and customer satisfaction, and the group was restored to financial health.

Selecting team members, designing team processes, ensuring cohesion by focusing on purposes and values, motivating people in order to create greater engagement: these are some of the tasks of leadership at team level. They are not easy, and there are no magic formulas or recipes for success. Each situation is different because the people themselves, along with their personalities and cultures and life experience and expectations, will always be different. Even teams that look very similar in terms of function and purpose will be quite different in terms of composition and personalities.

At team level, however, leaders have the advantage of being able to see their follower face to face, to talk with them and get to know them and to understand their individual needs and motivations and aspirations. When organisations become larger and more complex, that personal bond between leaders and followers is broken. As we shall see in the next chapter, the tasks of leadership become much harder.

FURTHER READING

Belbin, R. M., *Management Teams: Why They Succeed or Fail*, Routledge, 2010.

Edmondson, A., 'Psychological Safety and Learning Behavior in Work Teams', *Administrative Science Quarterly*, vol. 4, no. 2, 1999, pp. 350–383.

Goffee, R. and Jones, G., *Clever: Leading Your Smartest, Most Creative People*, Harvard Business Review Press, 2009.

Herzberg, F., 'One More Time: How Do You Motivate Employees?', *Harvard Business Review*, vol. 46, no. 1, 1968, pp. 53–62.

Janis, I.L., *Victims of Groupthink: A Psychological Study of Foreign-Policy Decisions and Fiascoes*, Houghton Mifflin, 1982.

Lewis, J.S., *Partnership for All*, Kerr-Cros Publishing, 1948.

Riggio, R.E., Chaleff, I. and Lipman-Blumen, J. (eds), *The Art of Followership: How Great Followers Create Great Leaders and Organizations*, Jossey-Bass, 2008.

Rousseau, D.M., *Psychological Contracts in Organizations: Understanding Written and Unwritten Agreements*, Sage, 1995.

Steiner, I.D., *Group Process and Productivity*, Academic Press, 1972.

White, A., *From Comfort Zone to Performance Management*, White & MacLean, 2009.

4

LEADERSHIP IN COMPLEX ORGANISATIONS

Leading small teams of ten or a dozen people is not the same as leading in larger organisations. All of the things discussed in the previous chapter are equally important, for example:

- Leaders still need followers to get things done.
- Getting the right people with the right skills into the right jobs or positions and enabling them to work together is crucial to effectiveness.
- Trust is essential if team members are to communicate and work as a unit.
- Diversity is an important source of creative thinking.
- Energy comes from both leaders and followers, and each influences the others.
- The strongest form of commitment comes when followers identify with the organisation and its values and work together willingly.

However, when organisations become larger, other factors intervene. First, there is the problem of time and space. In a small team decisions can be made quickly and enacted immediately, and the outcomes of those decisions can be monitored in real time: we know what progress we are making on the building of a new website, or the design of a new building, or whether we are winning or losing a game.

DOI: 10.4324/9781003496243-4

However, companies can employ tens of thousands or hundreds of thousands of people. Cities may have millions of people and nations are larger still, with tens or even hundreds of millions of inhabitants. Decision making takes longer, implementation takes longer still, and outcomes are much harder to monitor. If a mistake is made at a lower level, leaders at the top of the organisation may not know about it for a very long time – or ever.

The second intervening factor is complexity. We often use the words *complex* and *complicated* as interchangeable, but they mean two different things. Many large organisations are complicated, and doubtless could be simplified. But in large organisations, a degree of complexity is essential if they are to function effectively. This brings further challenges for leadership, and a fresh new set of paradoxes.

TIME AND SPACE: THE SPAN OF CONTROL

The people at the top of organisations – chairs and chief executives of businesses, mayors and prime ministers, generals and ship's captains – like to think that they control those organisations, and often speak as if they do. They take credit for the success of the organisation as if they were somehow solely responsible for it. In *War and Peace*, Leo Tolstoy again describes the Emperor Napoleon on the edge of a battlefield in Russia, unable to see anything thanks to clouds of smoke and reliant on messengers from the front to tell him what was going on. His ability to control the battlefield was virtually non-existent, and yet he still took credit for the victory.

You won't find the term 'one-leader fallacy' in any of the literature on leadership, or anything else, because I have just made it up. It is, nevertheless, a real thing. The idea is that every organisation has a single leader who is ultimately responsible for everything that happens in that organisation. When a trader in financial markets commits fraud, people believe that the chief executive of the bank that employs that trader should have known about the fraud and prevented it. When a government department makes a bad decision the prime minister is held responsible, despite the fact that most governments practise collective responsibility and the prime minister is expected to abide by the collective decision of colleagues; and so on.

Only very small organisations, a micro-business or a sports team, are able to get by with just one leader. In very large organisations there will be thousands of leaders, perhaps even tens of thousands. The reason for this is simple: leaders can directly manage only a very limited amount of what goes on around them. There is a limit to how far they can extend their direct authority, and the technical term for this limit is the *span of control.*

'Control' is perhaps a misleading term here. As the previous two chapters should have made clear, we don't control other people like robots, or put them together like Lego blocks. By control, what is meant here is the ability to observe, monitor, talk to and directly influence others and know with reasonable certainty what they are doing. If we ask them to undertake a task, we can see at once whether they are actually doing what is required and whether they are doing it correctly.

Anything outside of this span of control exists in a 'fog'. Leaders are unable to see clearly what is going on; like Napoleon in Russia, they can only guess at what is happening. Some leaders don't like to admit this, even to themselves, because accepting that they don't control the organisations that they lead would be damaging to their self-esteem: they would feel powerless and weak. Hence the persistence of the one-leader fallacy.

Even more damaging to leader's egos is the realisation that the span of control is actually very small. A.V. Graicunas, the Lithuanian engineer who first studied the concept back in the 1930s, reckoned that one person could 'control' no more than four other people. Subsequent research has suggested that the number is higher, perhaps eight to twelve people depending on context. We can see this principle in action in the sizes of many different teams. Sports teams typically have between six and twelve players in the field at any one time; in courtrooms, juries are usually composed of twelve people; ten to twelve members is considered the optimal size for the board of directors of firms; in the army, fire teams are usually eight to ten people, and so on.

THE PARADOX OF RESPONSIBILITY

Leaders are responsible for what happens in their organisations. Failure can result in them being demoted, losing their jobs altogether, fined and punished by regulators or even facing criminal charges. But the span of control means that they have very little direct control over the things for which they are responsible, and are unable to influence events until it is too late. Senior leaders are accountable for their organisations, but their real power over those organisations is often quite limited.

Direct communication with everyone on an individual basis is no longer possible. A moment of reflection will show why this is so. Imagine that you are in charge of an organisation of ten thousand people, and each of them sent you one email every day. It takes 2–3 minutes just to read an email of average length, so even if you did nothing but read emails for ten hours a day, it would take you nearly two months to get through just one day's accumulated messages. But if a leader can no longer communicate with every individual, they no longer have any direct control over what that person is doing or what their output is.

In very large organisations containing hundreds of thousands or more, leaders will never meet most of their followers. Indeed, they will not even be entirely certain how many followers they have. I once asked a number of senior leaders in a multinational corporation how many employees they had. None could give a precise figure, and estimates varied by as much as fifty thousand people. But this should not be surprising. In an organisation this size, people are joining or leaving all the time. The headcount will vary from one day to the next.

Added to this are the complications of physical space. Large companies, research organisations, international bodies like the UN's Food and Agriculture Organization or the WWF, the conservation charity, will have offices and facilities all around the globe. Until the nineteenth century, these large organisations could only communicate at the speed of the fastest boat or the fastest horse. The Hudson's

Bay Company, a British trading company in North America, was headquartered in London but had its main operational office at Fort Garry (the modern Canadian centre of Winnipeg) and dozens of trading posts scattered across an area of nearly four million square kilometres. If the governor wanted to know what was happening in these posts, he had to rely on letters or travel there himself. One governor in the early nineteenth century, Sir John Simpson, estimated that he travelled around fifty thousand kilometres a year, mostly in canoes or by dogsled.

Communications have improved, of course, and modern technology makes communications around the globe practically instantaneous, but this brings its own complications. First, technology has increased the volume of communications and data flows by several orders of magnitude. Artificial intelligence has the potential to help sift and digest information flows to make them more manageable, but leaders have to be careful not to become too dependent on AI. Technology can help us to make decisions, but it cannot make the decisions for us. Second, technology can provide senior leaders with an illusion of control. The notion that they can dial up anyone in the company and talk to them in real time convinces some leaders that they have overcome the limitations of the span of control. The reality, of course, is that the 'control' lasts for precisely the duration of the video call, after which the followers become invisible once more.

THE PARADOX OF THE FOG

The larger the organisation we lead, the less we can see of it. In small teams we can see and hear what the whole team are doing, but as the size grows from hundreds to thousands and tens of thousands, we see proportionally less. The organisation grows, but our vision remains the same as it was before.

For leaders of large organisations, the limitations of the span of control are one of the biggest obstacles they face. They can issue requests, instructions and orders, but they have no idea if their wishes are being respected or their orders carried out. For all they know, followers could be doing something entirely different to what is expected of them. And worse, the senior leaders won't know whether mistakes have been made or problems encountered until it is too late; sometimes, much too late. Monitoring real time date such as key performance indicators (KPIs) can be helpful, but it takes experience and skill to correctly interpret KPIs and know what story they are telling.

DISTRIBUTED LEADERSHIP

In order to run organisations larger than a handful of people, therefore, leaders rely on networks of other people. Companies have hierarchies of directors, country heads, division heads, department chiefs, senior managers, middle managers, team leaders and so on. Government departments have something similar. The armed forces and the police have senior, middle and junior ranks of officers to whom authority is devolved. A significant portion of any leader's job is to coordinate the other leaders around them. This leads us back to the paradox of power in Chapter 2: the more power you have, the more power you must give away in order to make that power effective. Power is distributed from senior leaders to other leaders throughout the organisation.

This distribution of leadership is essential if large organisations are to function. Each leader has their own team, and at management level each team member will also be a leader with *their* own team, and so on throughout the hierarchy of the organisation. We can see this very clearly in the armed forces: generals have teams of regimental commanders, each of whom has a team of company commanders, each of whom has a team of platoon commanders and so on, a system that goes back at least as far as the Roman Empire, if not further. Large companies will have directors with regional responsibility: the Americas, Asia, Europe-Middle East-Africa and so on, with teams of country directors, who in turn have teams of office and regional directors.

This means that no one has to read ten thousand emails a day. Followers report issues and problems to their leaders, who solve them locally where possible and, if not, report them in turn to their own leaders. The senior leaders should be kept aware of what is going on, but they should not interfere; they should leave the delegated leaders to solve their own problems and make their own decision, only stepping in if needed. With the delegation of power also comes a delegation of responsibility; the other leaders are responsible for their own areas.

Distribution of leadership, although necessary, creates problems:

- 'Other' leaders can conceal or fail to pass on important information from their own leaders, meaning that the more senior leaders remain unaware of problems in the organisation.
- Passing information along the chain takes time, which can be a weakness when quick responses are needed.
- In an organisation with hundreds or thousands of leaders at all levels, it can be difficult to know who has responsibility for what.
- Coordination between leaders and teams at the same level becomes difficult because they might not know where each other are or how to contact each other.

In the 1980s, complacent senior executives at computer maker IBM thought that their company was progressive and innovative with a culture of psychological safety where people were free to express their views. They did not realise that at lower levels of the company, psychological safety had vanished, meaning that dissent and creativity were being stifled and innovation had ground to a halt. Only when the company was on the edge of bankruptcy did the senior executives realise the truth.

TEAMS OF TEAMS

To deal with these problems, the temptation for leaders is to gather power into their own hands in hopes of establishing greater control, but the paradox of power tells us that this will not work. We need to think again about what control means. Mary Parker Follett, whom we mentioned earlier, argued in her book *Creative Experience* that the notion of control is itself an illusion, and that all of the things we think of as *control* are in reality forms of *coordination*.

Following this theme, later writers have described organisations as 'teams of teams' where small organisational units – teams – interlock with each other like bones in a skeleton or nodes in a network to form a larger organisation. Spotify, the Swedish-based audio streaming provider, uses this kind of structure with hundreds of small teams, known as 'squads', each organised around a particular task or function. The product-line teams we saw at Randalls in the previous chapter are another example.

This again leads us to think about complexity, but before we get into the subject, let us briefly consider three things that are needed to make this 'team of teams' model work:

- *A pipeline of capable leaders*. If we are going to have distributed leadership, we need to ensure that there are enough trained and motivated leaders who are capable of stepping into the required leadership positions. It has been said that the first job of a leader is to develop other leaders. All leaders should be trying to identify people in their teams who also have the potential and desire to become leaders.
- *Good communications*. In the previous chapter we talked about communications within teams, but we also need good communications between teams as well. We will come back to this in a moment.
- *Trust*. Trust is the antidote to the fog. Senior leaders may not know what other leaders in the organisation are doing, but if they can trust those leaders and know they are competent, they don't have to. The other leaders will get on with the job.

So:

- *What usually happens*: followers come to their leaders and say, 'I have a problem. How do I solve it?'
- *What should happen*: followers come to their leaders and say, 'I *had* a problem. This is how I solved it.'
- *What must not happen*: followers having problems and not saying anything to anyone.

Ideally, when leadership is shared and distributed, we want to see a climate where the second point happens as often as possible.

Leaders trust their followers to solve problems, and followers trust their leaders will give them the freedom to do so, and importantly, not punish them when they make mistakes. That last point is important. Followers *will* make mistakes, and so will leaders. We are only human, and even though we can use technology to try and reduce mistakes, the technologies have also been designed by fallible humans.

Blaming subordinates publicly and pointing the finger will damage self-esteem and reduce trust. If other people see that failures result in blame, they will be less likely to take risks themselves. Creativity will be bottled up and innovation will suffer. A better example is shown by Thomas Watson, chief executive of IBM in the 1950s. One of Watson's senior executives made a mistake that cost the company one hundred thousand dollars. The executive accepted responsibility and delivered his letter of resignation to Watson, who read the letter and tore it up. 'Aren't you going to fire me?' the executive asked. 'Why would I fire you?' Watson replied. 'I've just spent a hundred thousand dollars on your education.'

THE BATTLE OF CAEN

In the summer of 1346, early in the conflict later known as the Hundred Years' War, an English army under King Edward III landed in northern France. The English met little resistance at first, but they knew that the city of Caen in Normandy was heavily defended by a force led by a senior French commander, the Constable of France. As the English army approached Caen, King Edward gave his orders: scouts should be sent forward to study the French defences, but on no account should the army attack the city until the scouts had made their report and a plan of battle determined.

Going forward, the scouts at once found weaknesses in the French position. Quickly, they sent word to the nearest English companies: there was an opportunity here to break through the French defences. The company commanders agreed and sent their men into action. When King Edward heard of this, he sent the marshal of the

English army, the Earl of Warwick to remind the captains to obey orders.

When Warwick arrived on the scene, however, he found that the English were gaining ground and the French were giving way. He immediately cancelled the king's orders and brought more troops forward. Within a few hours Caen had been captured and the French commander was a prisoner in English hands. Although King Edward's orders had been broken repeatedly, the king praised Warwick and the captains for using their own initiative.

Warwick and the other captains could act as they did because the king trusted them to use their judgement, and they in turn trusted him to support them if they contravened his orders in order to get results. This trust was exhibited time and again throughout the ensuing campaign. On the other hand, King Edward's opponent, King Philip VI of France, did not trust his own officers and several times accused them in public of plotting against him. Fearing betrayal, he insisted that all orders had to come from him personally. The result was an inflexibility and inability to respond to threats that ultimately led to the French army to terrible defeat at the Battle of Crécy.

A team of teams, then, is an organisation where teams work harmoniously together in much the same manner as individuals work together in a team. This is easy to say but much harder to do. At Spotify, research has shown that the individual members of each 'squad' work together very well. Problems are more likely to rise when coordinating the work of squads with each other. Leading teams is relatively simple, compared to the complex task of leading teams of teams.

COMPLEXITY

In large organisations, complexity, like paradox, is something that leaders must live with. When confronted with complexity, there is often a strong temptation to simplify complex situations, or break down complex things into their component parts. Many of the management tools and frameworks we are taught at business schools or on training programmes are designed to do just that. This is a mistake because something that is truly complex cannot be simplified. It is complex because it has to be.

We use the terms *complex* and *complicated* interchangeably, but there is a difference. A thing that is complicated has unnecessary elements, parts that are not useful or may even be slowing things down. Imagine a device that has lots of apps whose function is not clear and are never used, but whose size and processing speed are slowing the rest of the device down. We would call this device complicated because it is clearly over-designed. In this case, deleting some of the useless apps will make the device work better and improve functionality.

In complex systems, however, every element has a role to play, and taking elements out of the system would damage functionality and decrease performance of the system. The modern study of complexity has its origins in fire control systems developed for ships during the Second World War, when ships would find themselves coming under attack by enemy aircraft coming from many different angles. Electro-mechanical fire control systems were designed which had the ability to detect aircraft, calculate course and speed very quickly and transmit this information to gun positions. These systems were complex because they had to be; if any of the detection systems or communications links were taken away, the system would be less effective.

Big organisations are complex because they must be. Companies will have many different subsidiaries, governments will have a lot of different departments and so on – and those subsidiaries will be further broken up into work units and teams – because this is the only way they can function. Because of the limitations on the span of control, we cannot have one big team working for one leader; that would be impossible. So, we must have hierarchies of teams, and teams within teams, operating within multiple spans of control.

But this poses challenges. As leaders, looking at these complex arrangements of teams, a question arises: how do we keep all of these different teams together? How do we prevent them from going off in their own direction, rather than working towards the needs of the wider organisation? By empowering people, we make them free: but does that mean making them free to do whatever they want?

THE PARADOX OF DIVISION AND COMBINATION

We find this paradox even at the level of individual teams: each team member has a specific role to play depending on their experience and expertise, but all need to work together. The eighteenth-century economist Adam Smith referred to this as the division and recombination of labour. For leaders, the challenge is this: how do we give individuals the freedom they need to do their jobs, while at the same time ensuring that they work together and conform to each other to achieve a common outcome? On the football field, how does the coach ensure that players play with freedom and use their own skills to the best effect, while at the same time playing as a team?

At the level of large and complex organisations, this paradox is amplified. How does a multi-national conglomerate business give a hundred subsidiaries in different sectors the freedom to pursue their own course, while at the same time ensuring that they are all working towards a common strategy? There is no answer to these questions, because this is a paradox. Leaders need to strike a balance between the two needs, but that balance will be constantly shifting and changing.

The answer lies in systems thinking. Two kinds of system are particularly important for leadership: *socio-technical systems* and *complex adaptive systems*. We will look at these now.

SOCIO-TECHNICAL SYSTEMS

The term socio-technical system (or sociotechnical system) was first developed in the mid-twentieth century and has been refined by subsequent research. Today the term is mostly used with reference to the relationship between people and technology, specifically how the former use the latter. Originally, though, the socio-technical system referred to the complex interrelationship between organisational structure and process and organisational culture and values.

Put simply, every organisation has two interlocking sub-systems: a *social sub-system* and a *technical sub-system*.

- The technical sub-system is the structure and processes. It includes the physical structure and hierarchy of the business as represented by organisation diagrams and process flow-charts, explaining how the parts of the business relate to each other. It also includes financial accounts that indicate business performance, articles of association, legal contracts that spell out responsibilities and rewards, technical handbooks and manuals, codes of conduct and other documents that, taken together, show how the organisation works together and what processes enable it to reach its goals. The technical sub-system is *explicit* and *codifiable*: that is, it is based on specific factual information and is easy to write down or put into visual diagrams and transmit to others.
- The social sub-system is the culture. It includes people's beliefs about the organisation and their own role in it, their relationships with other people in the organisation, their values and motivation, and also factors like trust and psychological safety. All of these things are largely invisible, which makes them difficult to define and transmit to others in any formal way; instead, it is the stories that people tell each other about their own feelings and experiences that, taken all together, create the social system. The social sub-system can be summed up as what people feel about the organisation, each other, and themselves.

These two sub-systems are inseparable; they are like the two sides of a coin, or the light side and dark side of the moon. Every organisation has both a formal technical design and a largely invisible culture based on beliefs and stories. We can change the technical structure by reorganising, we can influence people's beliefs and values for better or worse, but we cannot do away with them entirely. Even if we got rid of all hierarchies and boundaries, all divisions and departments and teams and made everyone equal, the result would still be a structure.

From a leadership perspective, we need to recognise the following:

1. We are leading both sub-systems at the same time, and
2. We need to lead *both* sub-systems so they are in sync with each other.

Point 2 is particularly important. Here is why:

- An organisation with a *strong technical sub-system* and a *weak social sub-system* will be technically efficient at what it does, but the people in the organisation will lack motivation and belief, have few or weak values and be uninterested in collaborating with each other. Each person will be there for what they get out of the organisation, while putting in as little as possible. At best, productivity will decline; at worst, the door to corruption and theft is opened. And without commitment, technical systems will not be fully used and will begin to decline.
- An organisation with a *weak technical sub-system* and a *strong social sub-system* will be filled with people who are committed and keen, ready to work together and wanting to reach their mutually shared goals. But if the organisation is divided into silos that impede communications, or if the technical structure is weak and people are not really sure what their roles are and what they are meant to do, or if there is lack of clarity over responsibility and reward, that early commitment and motivation will rapidly erode. As we saw in the last chapter, motivation theory suggests that 'hygiene' factors in the workplace environment, things like working conditions, pay and management quality, can be demotivating. As motivation and commitment fades, the organisation will slide into the worst of all possible worlds: a weak technical sub-system and, now, a weak social sub-system as well.
- By contrast, an organisation with a *strong technical sub-system* and a *strong social sub-system* has elements that are necessary for success: efficient structure, functioning processes and good communications that enable committed and motivated followers to reach their goals.

The technical sub-system feels like the easiest one to deal with. We can see this system, describe it in documents and diagrams, and measure and observe how well it is working. If something is going wrong we can change the system: we can restructure the organisation, redesign processes, rewrite contracts, bring in more resources, move people from one department or regional office to another. We might even decide to break up the organisation into separate parts, like the leaders of General Electric who, in 2024, split the corporation into three separate companies focused on different areas of activity.

The social sub-system is harder to deal with because so much of it is intangible. Changing the culture of an organisation is often said to be the hardest task in leadership, time-consuming and with no guarantees of success. When performance is declining or things are going wrong within the organisation, the temptation is to change the technical system because that is easiest and (supposedly) most straightforward. But if changes to the technical system are out of step with the social system, not only will performance not improve, it might even get worse. The example of Alliance Airlines (below) illustrates this.

ALLIANCE AIRLINES

Alliance Airlines (not its real name) is an American airline flying a variety of domestic and international routes. The social sub-system at Alliance was very strong and staff motivation levels were high. Employees cared deeply about their jobs and the company had strong values based around service to customers and creating value for them. If customers had problems, airline staff were always ready to step in and help. As a result the airline had many loyal customers who chose Alliance over all the other competing airlines.

A new chief executive took charge of the company, with instructions from the shareholders to increase profits. The CEO looked at the technical sub-system and saw that while the airline had strong revenues, it was also employing very large numbers of people. Costs were also high, particularly the training budget. To save money, the CEO decreed that several hundred employees would be made redundant and the training budget, which he did not believe was an essential expenditure, would be cut to 10 per cent of its former level.

Both of these measures improved technical efficiency, but they eroded the social sub-system. Employees at Alliance really valued the training programmes they received, which equipped them with new skills and were also a chance to socialise and develop relationships with colleagues. The loss of training, coupled with the departure of so many of their colleagues, reduced morale and broke the bonds of trust between followers and leaders. With so many of their friends being made redundant, people wondered if their turn might be next.

Employee motivation declined, and people started to care less about their jobs. They stopped going the extra mile to help customers, and customer service levels declined. Disappointed by the service they received, previously loyal customers began switching to other airlines. Revenues and profits fell, and the company's financial position deteriorated to the point where, eighteen months later, Alliance Airlines filed for protection from bankruptcy.

Apparently minor changes by the leader to the technical sub-system did profound damage to the social sub-system and ultimately broke the company. The lesson is that *any* change to the social sub-system could impact on the technical sub-system, and vice versa.

COMPLEX ADAPTIVE SYSTEMS

Writers on complexity sometimes talk about two forms of complexity:

1. *Disorganised complexity*, where all the parts in a system move apparently at random; examples include the movement of galaxies, or the movement of sub-atomic particles.
2. *Organised complexity*, where all the parts move in predictable ways as part of a coherent system; examples include ant colonies and beehives, and the human brain.

Systems with organised complexity are known as *complex adaptive systems*. Here are some of the features of a complex adaptive system with examples of how they apply to organisations:

- The ability to self-organise.
- Synergy.
- Self-regulation.

- Communication and cooperation.
- Adaptive capacity

We will now look at each of these in more detail.

THE ABILITY TO SELF-ORGANISE

Distributed leadership means that individual elements of the organisation have the ability to change and adapt to circumstances. If a threat arises, people and resources are moved and new teams are formed to meet it and put up resistance. If an opportunity appears, the organisation reconfigures itself to take advantage. All of this is done locally, without the need to seek permission from other authorities.

Self-organisation works when top leadership makes it clear to the other levels of leadership that they are trusted and are expected to make their own decisions. Psychological safety is also important here; other leaders need to know that they can take risks, within reason, and that they will not be punished if they sometimes fail. Senior leaders need to expect that failures will happen from time to time, and that this is part of the process. Some failures can be tolerated so long as there are gains as well.

Of course there are limits to this. Risks that could endanger other organisations or the entire company would not be tolerated, and repeated failures would be a clear sign that something is wrong. Senior leaders need to be clear about the organisation's *risk appetite*, what levels of risk are acceptable and what are not. For example, in a hospital it would be acceptable to take risks around designing new procedures or bringing in new equipment, provided that patients were not being put unnecessarily in danger.

Self-organisation also requires clarity of purpose across the whole organisation. Leaders can use power that is distributed to them so long as they do so in ways that are congruent with the wider organisation's purpose and goals. To return to the hospital example, organising a new team to improve sanitation and reduce the risk of infection would be in line with the hospital's goals.

MCKINSEY & COMPANY

McKinsey & Company is a large management consulting firm specialising in strategy and organisation. Founded in the USA in the 1920s, from the 1960s onward McKinsey began expanding overseas. Today McKinsey has offices in over sixty countries.

McKinsey's expansion was rarely planned and was largely a result of local leaders spotting opportunities and taking advantage of them. If a partner in the firm believed there was an opportunity to open a new office in a particular city or country, they would tell their office manager and the two of them would discuss whether there was likely to be enough business to support a new office and what resources would be needed. Head office in New York would be kept informed, and senior managers might offer advice and comment, but there was no formal approval process. The ultimate decision about whether to open a new office was left to the partners themselves.

Once the new office was established, it was again down to the partners to decide whether the venture was working. If after a period of time – usually a year – not enough business was coming in, the partner in charge would wind up the venture and return to their base office. If business was good, the office would be formally established and new staff brought in. In some cases the partners at the new office would identify another opportunity and move there as well. All of this happened organically, with decisions made locally and little or no interference from head office.

SYNERGY

Synergy, sometimes also known as *emergence*, comes about when people working together are able to be more productive than when they are working on their own. The economist Adam Smith wrote about this in his classic book, *An Inquiry into the Nature and Causes of the Wealth of Nations*. He described how workers making metal pins could, when working on their own, manage to make a few pins a day. Working as a team, however, they could make thousands of pins every day. The difference between the efforts of the individuals and the efforts of the team is synergy.

Synergy can happen at all levels, between individual teams, between departments and between organisations. It requires people to work together and communicate with each other, sharing knowledge and skills. It also requires that they understand the purpose of their work and what they are meant to do.

Unless people are sufficiently motivated to work together, synergy is unlikely to emerge. Instead we find its opposite, *social loafing*, where people do not work to their full capacity and team productivity falls away. Sociologists first identified social loafing when studying team sports, specifically tug-of-war contests. They found in single-person contests with one person on each end of the rope trying to pull the other off their feet, each player would put one hundred per cent of their effort into trying to win. In teams of four, however, not everyone would pull as hard as they could, counting on others around them to do the work instead. Later research has identified similar effects in work teams.

Ensuring that synergy is created and social loafing is avoided is difficult for senior leaders because they are not close enough to the workplace. They have to rely on distributed leadership, giving authority to team leaders and others closer to the working teams to ensure this is done. However, senior leaders have a role to play in encouraging synergy by motivating the whole organisation. Senior leaders remind everyone of the purpose and mission, what the organisation is doing and why. This provides a vital element in encouraging synergy, while team leaders lower down in the organisation work to ensure good communications and teamworking practices.

Senior leaders also create synergy between organisations. No organisation exists in a vacuum; all have partnerships with other organisations. Companies, for example, work with suppliers, distributors, retailers, providers of services such as IT and accountancy. They also have to deal with customers, shareholders, banks and a variety of other stakeholders. Senior leaders have an important role to play in maintaining relationships with these organisations, and they might also create partnerships with other businesses to take advantage of opportunities. Educational and healthcare institutions might create partnerships for research or to advance particular causes.

INTERNATIONAL COMMITTEE OF THE RED CROSS

In 1863 the Swiss businessman Henri Dunant founded the Geneva Welfare Society for the purpose of providing medical aid to wounded soldiers, and to campaign for international treaties to protect both the wounded and the medical workers who cared for them. Dunant and his colleagues realised that as a single society their reach and impact would be limited, so in October of 1863 they held an international conference with representatives from eighteen national governments and a number of other organisations. This led to the First Geneva Convention, an international agreement governing the care and treatment of wounded soldiers and civilians.

Other countries began founding their own humanitarian societies, but they needed a coordinating mechanism for international cooperation. The original society transformed into the International Committee of the Red Cross (ICRC) in 1876 and became the international governing body. Today the ICRC continues to play an important role in helping national Red Cross organisations and other humanitarian agencies work together and create synergy.

SELF-REGULATION

Also known as homeostasis, self-regulation means that the different parts of the organisation work together automatically, without conscious direction. The human body is a useful metaphor. The various organs, muscles and bones of the body function normally without us having to give them orders; we do not have to tell ourselves to breathe, or order the heart to pump blood, or instruct our feet to move in order to walk. Another important aspect of self-regulation is the ability of the parts to repair themselves. If we cut our finger, for example, unless the wound is very deep or becomes infected, the cut will heal and the body will return to normal.

Self-regulation happens in organisations when all of the parts know their purpose and are working together with the other parts. There are similarities to synergy, but with the additional difference that if there is a threat to one part of the organisation, other parts will come to its assistance. For example, if a project team runs into difficulties that threaten to delay implementation, it can call on other teams for help. The request for help doesn't need to be channelled back to head office and no senior leadership approval. The request happens automatically.

Research organisations commonly have this element, but in other types of firm where there is more an emphasis on linear processes – assembly lines in automobile plants, for example – self-regulation can be harder to achieve. Once again, the solution lies in devolution of authority and power. Local leaders need to be empowered to step in where necessary and offer help and resources when other leaders and teams are struggling. This ensures a rapid response and more effective problem solving.

CARL ZEISS

The firm of Carl Zeiss was established in the German city of Jena in the late nineteenth century. Originally a maker of scientific instruments, the firm later focused on making optical lenses of very high quality, and associated instruments such as cameras, binoculars, microscopes and telescopes. The firm had a global reputation for quality and its products were sold around the world.

Ernst Abbe, the managing director, seldom gave direct orders to his teams. He was in constant contact with his team leaders, but his purpose was usually to find out what they wanted to work on next and what resource they would need in terms of technology and people, and then provide those resources. Everyone at Carl Zeiss knew what the firm's purpose was: to create products of the very highest quality that would sustain the firm's reputation, and provide accurate instruments that other people needed to carry out their own work as scientists, photographers, film-makers, surveyors and so on. Their pride in their work was immense.

As a result, if a team ran into a problem when developing a new project, team members knew they could always call on other teams and departments for help. Ernst Abbe let it be known that this was the behaviour he expected, and then stepped back. The people themselves did the rest.

COMMUNICATION AND COOPERATION

Self-regulation relies on communication and feedback between different parts of the organisation. We saw in the example of the anti-aircraft fire control systems how important communication is. Earlier we referred to communication within teams, but communication between teams is equally important, perhaps even more so.

In complex organisations, leaders still have to communicate with followers. As noted, they need to remind followers about the purpose and mission and motivate them to work towards the common goals. They also need to ensure that followers are communicating with each other, and this is largely done through distributed leadership, expecting and encouraging other leaders to ensure smooth communications among their teams.

Along with communication comes cooperation. Self-regulation also relies on the willingness of people within the organisation to cooperate and share knowledge. To ensure this is done, senior leadership needs to create and reinforce a culture of trust and psychological safety. Once again, this is largely done by setting expectations for other leaders and encouraging them to contribute to that culture.

Leading by example is extremely important here. In large organisations, leaders set the tone. They may not see their followers, but they must put themselves in positions where their followers can see them. As Robert Cialdini explains in his book, *Influence*, leaders are also influencers: their followers look to them for guidance and example. If the leaders are visibly seen to be trusting and empowering others, trust and empowerment begin to seem normal and others will follow their example.

THE DEVELOPMENT OF COVID-19 VACCINES

The development of new medical products is a long and slow process. It can take ten years, sometimes longer, for a new product to move from the initial development stage to reach the market. So when the Covid-19 pandemic broke out in 2020, the prospects for a vaccine to protect people looked bleak.

Instead, the medical research community showed what it can do when cooperation and communication are present. Research labs, medical facilities, pharmaceutical companies, university departments and governments around the world collaborated. Results of analyses and attempts to sequence the DNA of the virus were widely shared. Pharmaceutical companies competed with each other, racing to see which could produce a vaccine first, but they also shared information with each other. A process which usually takes many years was reduced to a matter of months.

There was no central leadership guiding the process. The World Health Organization helped to coordinate the various organisations involved, but did not lead the research. Leadership was collective and collaborative. It existed in the space between these organisations, not within any one organisation itself.

ADAPTIVE CAPACITY

The ability of any organisation to survive and prosper depends in large part on its ability to adapt to changing circumstances, to respond to threats and take advantage of opportunities. One of the leader's concerns must be to ensure that the organisation has adaptive capacity and can react quickly. Many famous companies failed because of a lack of adaptive capacity. Kodak, which had dominated the world camera market for decades, failed to adapt to the change to digital photography and disappeared from the market very quickly. IBM, which had specialised in the market for large mainframe computers, was caught off guard when microcomputers entered the market, and never recovered its position; today, IBM no longer makes computers at all.

Leaders ensure that adaptive capacity exists by doing two things. The first is called *horizon scanning*. Leaders need to study the wider environment and look for new trends and technologies, signs of things to come. At time of writing, for example, artificial intelligence (AI) offers both opportunities and challenges. How will AI impact on the future of the organisation?

The second thing is to ensure that the other elements of the complex adaptive system are in place. Self-organisation, synergy, self-regulation, communication and cooperation are all essential ingredients. Andrew Grove, the former leader of computer chip maker Intel, stressed that a combination of horizon scanning and flexible, reactive organisation was critical when facing a crisis. Only knowledgeable, flexible organisations would survive. But those same qualities can also be very important when taking up new opportunities, as the next case example shows.

THE MEDICI BANK

The Medici Bank started in Florence in the late fourteenth century as a small bank, and went on to become a diversified conglomerate involved in banking, trade, manufacturing and mining. It was the largest business in Europe, with operations in all major cities and agency relationships as far away as Iceland and China.

The Bank is an excellent example of a complex adaptive organisation. The structure was a series of interlocking partnerships – at the bank's largest extent, more than a hundred of these – each with three to five partners. Some partners contributed investment, while others might bring specialist knowledge of a particular line of business or location. Partnerships were established by contract and lasted for two or three years.

At the end of each contract, the partners analysed performance. If the partnership was doing well and making money, they signed a new contract, again for a period of two or three years. If change was required, some partners exited and new ones were brought in. Or, if the business was perceived to have run its course, the partnership was dissolved and the partners went on to other things. Furthermore, each partner was also a member of more than one partnership within the firm. Some were members of four or five partnerships at the same time.

The following features of a complex adaptive organisation can be seen:

Self-organisation: partnerships were organised locally by entrepreneurs. Some were members of the firm, but outsiders could also be brought in. Head office in Florence did not direct the formation of these partnerships, although it would intervene if failing partnerships were not dissolved.

Synergy: the presence of partners in more than one partnership created a network that enabled partnerships in different business lines and different cities to work together.

Self-regulation: partners were responsible for governing their own affairs. Head office rarely intervened, at least so long as profits were being generated.

Communication and cooperation: head office did sponsor an excellent courier service, and a special code for the transmission of documents. This along with the network of partnerships described above ensured good lateral communication through the firm.

Adaptive capacity: the Medici Bank, despite its size, could move rapidly to take advantage of business opportunities across Europe. Medieval businesses worked with very high levels of risk, but in times of crisis the partnerships could easily support each other.

THE COMPLEX ADAPTIVE SYSTEM AND THE SOCIO-TECHNICAL SYSTEM

A complex adaptive system will involve both sides of the socio-technical system, as follows:

Self-organisation	Social: mutual bonds of trust between head office and locations
	Technical: good systems for reporting and analysing information
Synergy	Social: willingness to work together, enabled by trust
	Technical: processes that enable team working to perform well
Self-regulation	Social: mutual support between different elements
	Technical: the ability to transfer people and resources where needed
	Communication and cooperation Social: inclusion and psychological safety leading to trust

	Technical: communications channels that enable people to exchange knowledge and skills
Adaptive capacity	Social: a culture that embraces change and challenge
	Technical: systems that process information quickly to detect threats and spot opportunities

To get the most out of these systems leaders need to do two things. First, they need to accept that the social and technical sub-systems are inseparable, and be able to manage both at once. Second, they need to create organisational systems that are able to self-organise, achieve synergy, regulate themselves, communicate and adapt.

If they can do these things, leadership becomes comparatively easier. If the system effectively runs itself, leadership becomes a matter of monitoring what is going on and intervening where needed, while concentrating on issues like strategy and future direction. The less time they have to spend managing the organisation, the more time they will have for horizon scanning and anticipating future challenges.

THE PARADOX OF NOW AND THEN

Leaders need to be looking to the future to try and chart a direction for the organisation, but they also need to be monitoring what is going on in the present. Neglect the former, and the organisation could be ambushed by unexpected change; neglect the latter and they could fall into the same trap as the bosses of IBM, unaware of what is going on in their organisations until it is too late. Leading is like walking with one eye on the ground underfoot and the other eye watching the horizon: necessary, but very difficult to do.

VALUES-DRIVEN SYSTEMS

We have talked a lot about values, but we haven't really defined them until now. Values, like leadership itself, is a fuzzy concept that can be hard to pin down. Essentially, values are the things we believe in. They influence our perceptions of right and wrong. They are the basis on which we approve – or disapprove – of the actions of other people. Research in psychology tells us that we are more likely to be attracted to people whose values are similar to our own, and more likely to trust them and follow them as well.

One of the things that any leader needs to do is identify clearly what their own values are and demonstrate those values to followers. This is particularly true in large and complex organisations. To repeat the point above, leaders don't see all of their followers: they may not know the names of followers or anything else about them. But the followers will be aware of the leaders and will be watching them, trying to form their own estimations of who the leader is and what they stand for.

As a leader, talking about your values and telling other people what your values are is not enough. Those values must be lived and enacted. This is known as 'walking the walk': behaving in ways that show what your values are. If you say you are trustworthy, you must keep your promises. If you say that you do not tolerate bullying or abuse, you must not behave in ways that are perceived as bullying or abusive, and you must deal firmly with others that do behave badly.

It is not necessary for your values and those of your followers to be identical. Everyone's values are different, even if subtly so. Followers will respect you for the conviction and sincerity with which you as a leader hold your values as much as for the values themselves. But they will identify your views as being the same as the organisation's values: in their minds, what you stand for and what the organisation stands for will be the same thing.

And while values will differ, there nevertheless needs to be some congruence. Followers don't have to always have the same values: they can feel differently about social issues, vote for different political parties and so on, but so long as the organisation is concerned, they need to share the organisation's values. One of the leader's tasks is to communicate what those values are – yours and the organisation's – and invite followers to share those values willingly. Those who are not willing to do so need to be asked to respect the values of others, or if they are not willing to do so, to exit the organisation. This may sound unfair, but clashing sets of values within an organisation can do a great deal of damage.

Values influence energy and motivation. People who feel that their values line up with the values of the organisation will work harder and be more productive. They will also often be happier and have higher self-esteem. The leader's job is to protect and preserve the values so that people will continue to share them.

VALUES OF SERVICE AND TRUST: THE TATA GROUP

We have mentioned the Tata Group already and seen the values of its founder, Jamsetji Tata, who believed that what comes from the people should go back to the people. Tata was an Indian patriot. He believed the British rule in India would one day come to an end, although he did not live to see it, and that a free India would need a strong economy to create prosperity for its people. Tata's business ventures in manufacturing, steel, hotel, electric power generation and so on were founded with this goal in mind.

Those values were perpetuated by Jamsetji's successors, especially JRD Tata through the twentieth century and Ratan Tata into the twenty-first. Trust and service to the community were identified as core values. Tata did not exist to make money: its purpose was to create value for the people. It did, and does, make money because its operations are efficient and effective. In the words of R. Gopalakrishnan, the former deputy chair of the group, 'profit is a by-product of what we do.'

The Tata Group did not just express these values, it lived them through programmes of community support, education and healthcare provision, support for women's rights and female entrepreneurs and a host of other programmes across India. At Jamshedpur in the state of Jharkhand, where soils are poor and making a living from the land is very difficult, Tata Steel provides free primary education and healthcare to the inhabitants of several hundred villages in the area. Tata Chemicals provides free consultancy advice to farmers. Titan, the watchmaker, gives grants to employees who leave and want to set up their own businesses.

The most spectacular example of the Tata Group living its values came in 2004 when a new subsidiary, Tata Finance, collapsed with massive financial losses. Many of the people who lost money were families and pensioners who stood to lose all of their savings. Ratan Tata, the chair, pledged publicly to repay every rupiah that had been lost; no one would lose money. He later said that at the time, he did not know how much money had been lost, and he made the promise prepared if necessary to liquidate the entire group and sell all of its assets in order to repay the bank's customers. 'If we had not made that promise, no one would ever have trusted us again', he said. 'And everything we had worked for would have been thrown away.' That is what is meant by walking the walk.

COMPLEXITY AND LEADERSHIP

Very little is certain in leadership, and in larger organisations there is even less certainty: recall the paradox of the fog from Chapter 2. Nick Obolensky's book *Complex Adaptive Leadership* talks about the need for leaders to not shy away from complexity and to embrace its principles.

The most important aspect of complexity that leaders need to consider is the need to think holistically. Management tools and frameworks teach us to break systems down into their parts, but we cannot break complexity down. If we try to do so, we lose sight of the whole.

Consider a tree growing in the forest. If we wanted to examine this tree, we could cut it down, strip away the leaves and bark and analyse them, slice up the trunk and count the rings in the wood to determine its age, dig up the roots to determine the source of nutrients and so on. We could learn a lot about the parts of the tree, but it would no longer be a tree. We can't stick the parts back together again.

Similarly, we cannot lead little bits of an organisation and leave the rest to its own devices. When we distribute power to other leaders, we are sharing that power with them, not turning our back on them and leaving them alone. We are responsible for the entire organisation and its people, and they look to us for leadership guidance. A leader cannot control ten thousand people, or ten million, but they can exercise leadership through influence and example. We will come back to this point in Chapter 6.

Next, however, we need to put leadership into context. Above, we noted that leadership is situational and that context matters. Let's now look at how and why it matters, and the implications for leadership.

FURTHER READING

Cialdini, R.B., *Influence: The Psychology of Persuasion*, Harper Business, 2021.

Fidanboy, M., *Organizations and Complex Adaptive Systems*, Routledge, 2024.

Grove, A., *Only the Paranoid Survive: How to Exploit the Crisis Points that Challenge Every Company and Career*, Profile Books, 2022.

Kraemer, H.M.J., *From Values to Action: The Four-Principles of Value-Based Leadership*, Wiley, 2025.

Maio, G.R., *The Psychology of Human Values*, Routledge, 2016.

McChrystal, S., Collins, T., Silverman, D. and Fussell, C., *Team of Teams: New Rules of Engagement for a Complex World*, Penguin, 2015.

Obolensky, N., *Complex Adaptive Leadership: Embracing Paradox and Uncertainty*, Routledge, 2024.

Pasmore, W.A., *Designing Effective Organizations: The Sociotechnical Systems Perspective*, Wiley, 1988.

Stacey, R.D. and Mowles, C., *Strategic Management and Organisational Dynamics: The Challenge of Complexity to Ways of Thinking About Organisations*, Pearson, 2015.

5

SITUATION AND CONTEXT IN LEADERSHIP

Situational leadership was formally defined by Paul Hersey and Ken Blanchard in the 1970s and 1980s. Their research found that the most effective leaders are those who are capable of adapting to rapidly to new situations, both within their own organisations and when switching between organisations. Different cultures, different times and different places call for different approaches to leadership, and history is full of examples of leaders who succeeded in one organisation but failed to adapt to the needs of their next role. John Sculley was highly successful as the chief executive of soft drink maker PepsiCo, but he struggled to adapt to a similar role at Apple Computers. Sir Clive Woodward coached the England rugby union team that won the World Cup in 2003, but his tenure as a manager at Southampton football club was widely regarded as a failure.

However, other leaders do adapt to new situations. George Washington, referred to earlier, was a successful general who became an equally successful president of the new American republic. Lou Gerstner held leadership roles in management consultancy, banking and finance and food production companies before becoming CEO at computer firm IBM and masterminding the company's turnaround following near-bankruptcy. Dame Sarah Mullally was chief nurse in the National Health Service before joining the clergy and becoming Archbishop of Canterbury.

DOI: 10.4324/9781003496243-5

But situation and context can still have an impact within a single organisation. For example, a business which had dominated its sector might suddenly run into difficulties when disruptive new technologies emerge, such as the case of Kodak mentioned in the previous chapter. Similarly, Blockbuster, a video rental chain which had developed a very successful business renting films on tape or DVD was caught out by the development of the internet and access to films very cheaply through streaming. In both cases, the leadership lacked sufficient adaptive capacity to adjust to the new situation. At time of writing, firms in many sectors are struggling similarly to adapt to the development of generative AI.

These are leadership issues because leaders, while standing back and giving their teams the space in which to create value, also need to be watching out for the overall health of the organisation and any trends from outside that might present a threat. When problems arise, the leader works with the team to overcome them; when opportunities are spotted, the leader informs the team and they consider how to respond. But in order to be effective, leaders need to be able to adapt to new situations, to recognise what is changing and to know how to respond.

What makes the difference between those who can adapt and those who cannot? Much attention has been focused on the qualities of leaders themselves and what makes them adaptable. Certainly there are important qualities that a leader needs, including empathy with others, an interest in new things and a willingness to learn. We will discuss these in this chapter, but there is more to this issue than just personal attributes.

This brings us back to the concept of the *leadership space*. How well a leader succeeds in a new environment is dependent largely on the relationship between the leader and their followers, how well they communicate and work together. Here, we will consider that relationship and the concepts of adaptability and adaptive capacity in three contexts: culture, time and space.

CULTURE

There is an old saying that 'culture eats strategy for breakfast', meaning that culture is such a powerful force in organisations that it can prevent even the best strategies from being implemented. Culture has chewed up and spat out a few leaders too. The merger of American technology company Lucent and French telecommunications provider Alcatel Alsthom in 2006 was badly affected by a clash of cultures between the French and American parts of the company. That clash was exemplified by the personal disputes between the chief executive Patricia Russo, who had been CEO of Lucent, and chair of the board Serge Tchuruk, who had been CEO of Alcatel Alsthom. Both were eventually forced to resign and the company was taken over by a rival firm, Nokia.

Culture is another of those concepts that can be hard to define and pin down. At its heart, culture is the beliefs and perceptions that people have of their organisations and themselves. The values are part of the culture, but so too are processes, ways of doing things that the organisation has developed over time. Sometimes these differences are quite subtle, but they can have profound impacts. An army officer who had worked on a joint project with a local government body once told me of how he struggled to understand his civilian colleagues and their priorities. His summary of the difference was succinct: 'In the army, we agree the plan, get the job done and then have a cup of tea. Our colleagues in government agreed the plan, had a cup of tea and then started working on the job.'

For our purposes in this book, culture exists across three levels:

1. *National cultures*: the culture of a nation or country and how it affects the behaviours of leaders and followers. Many nations will also have regional sub-cultures.
2. *Industry or sector cultures*: individual sectors will have their own established terminologies, symbols and ways of doing things. Examples include financial services, entertainment and software.
3. *Organisational cultures*: each organisation has its own culture, and again, there will often be many sub-cultures within the larger whole.

At every level, much of culture is symbolic, although the nature of the symbols may change depending on the level. People attach meaning to certain things in their environment: names, objects, flags, songs, buildings and of course, people. At management consultants McKinsey & Company, the firm's values have a strong symbolic presence: walk into any McKinsey office in the world and within a few minutes you will see a list of the values portrayed on a wall or screen: *Client first, firm second, self third.* In the Tata Group every office will have photographs or sculptures of the founder, Jamsetji Tata, displayed prominently, reminding everyone of the group's values and heritage.

But culture is also dynamic, and it changes, sometimes in unwelcome ways. Recall the example of Alliance Airlines in the previous chapter, and how the culture changed dramatically in the wake of cuts to the training budget. That cut sent a signal to staff: top leadership no longer cares about you. That was not the intention behind the cuts, but that nonetheless was how staff interpreted the move. Culture may be powerful, but it is also fragile and easy to damage.

CANADIAN ARMED FORCES

The Canadian army played an important role in the First World War, and all three services, army, navy and air force, were prominent in the Second World War. Canadian units also served in the Korean conflict and contributed many units to United Nations peacekeeping forces. The navy and air force were rewarded with the addition of 'royal' to their title, becoming the Royal Canadian Navy and the Royal Canadian Air Force. Many individual units had proud traditions and battle honours.

In 1964, a proposal was put forward to unify all three services into a single organisation to be called the Canadian Armed Forces. The old uniforms would be scrapped and all three services would wear the same uniform and have the same ranks, The primary reason was to save costs, although the government also expected that there would be improvements in coordination between the three services.

The proposal met with widespread protests. It was felt that the old traditions of the three services would be lost, and the common uniform would mean that each service would lose its distinctive identity. Senior officers pushed back against the proposal, and the government responded by dismissing the head of the navy and forcing other officers into retirement. The three services were finally merged in 1968, but the hoped-for savings and coordination benefits were more than offset by the loss of morale and motivation. In 2011 the government finally admitted that a mistake had been made. The old names for the three services were restored, and although the common uniform remained, different badges for each branch of service were brought in.

The protests were not so much about the merger itself, and more about the loss of things like uniforms and ranks and unit names, which were symbols of a heritage on which the culture of each service was built. The proposal made sense from a utilitarian perspective, but it did a great deal of damage to the culture.

There is an open debate about whether leaders can control the culture of organisations. David Knight and Hugh Willmott in their textbook *Introducing Organizational Behaviour and Management* make the point that leaders would quite like to control culture and will attempt to do so by manipulating variables that could change culture. An example is changing reward structures. If leaders want followers to change their behaviour, they might explain what new behaviours are desired and then reward those followers who are willing to change with bonuses, gifts, extra holidays, places on training programmes and so on.

However, there is real doubt as to how effective these manipulating efforts really are. Changing reward structures, for example, could be seen as 'bribing' employees to behave in certain ways, and this could cause resentment. Oracle, the American software company, reportedly tried to encourage a more aggressive attitude among its sales force by paying additional bonuses to those who brought in the most business. These extra bonuses were paid in the form of gold bars. This provoked a backlash both inside the company and in the wider community; the payments in gold in particular were seen as encouraging greed. The company soon dropped the idea.

The alternative view is that leaders can't control culture, because a lot of culture-building is done by the followers, the other members of the organisation who share experiences and perceptions of the organisation – and its leadership – often in the form of stories. Social media had amplified the ability of followers to create culture in this way: chat groups, often invisible to the leadership, mean that good and bad experiences can be shared quickly across even very large organisations.

THE PARADOX OF CULTURE

Leaders influence the culture of organisations, but they are also part of the culture. Robert Cialdini in his book *Influence* tells us that people are more likely to imitate the actions of other people whom they respect. Conversely, though, people will actively try to avoid behaving like people whom they do *not* respect. Leaders will try to influence the culture, but the perceptions by others will be transmitted around the organisation and will become part of the culture, often in ways the leaders did not intend.

Instead of controlling culture, therefore, leaders should aim instead for *influence*. Robert Cialdini describes several ways that leaders can influence the culture of their organisations:

- *Reciprocity*. People have a natural inclination to return favours. If leaders do favours for their followers, therefore, the latter are more likely to respond positively. The 'favour' could take the form of a bonus or other financial reward, but it could also be something that the follower wants for personal reasons: more responsibility, a chance for training and personal development, or even just public recognition. Even saying 'thank you' can make people feel more connected to the organisation and more responsive to leadership.
- *Consistency*: most of us, most of the time, are not fond of change. When things change we feel uncertain, because we

don't know what the future holds or how it will impact on us. Leaders who can provide consistency are more likely to attract people to follow them. Paradoxically, this is even more true in times when the organisation needs to change. The change message needs to delivered in a consistent way, with the message that either a) the changes will be positive, and/or b) some things will also remain the same, so people still have something solid to reassure them.

- *Social proof*: people are more likely to do something if they see someone else doing it. The negative side of this is the herd instinct where people follow others blindly, even into risk and danger. More positively, if leaders set a positive example, they increase the likelihood that others will follow that example. Here again we can learn from how other influencers gain followings through tactics like consistency, repetition of the message, establishing connections with followers and so on.
- *Authority*: Cialdini argues that people are likely to follow other people who are in positions of authority. This is true up to a point (and arguably less true now than it was when Cialdini was writing, as perceptions of authority have changed in many cultures). There are also many others who will challenge authority if they don't like what authority is perceived to stand for, as recent protest movements in countries as diverse as the USA, Bangladesh and Iran continue to show. The caveat the needs to be added is: people are more likely to follow other people in positions of authority *if the people trust those authority figures*. Otherwise they are likely to ignore them or actively oppose them. Genuine authority is founded on trust.
- *Liking*: people are also more likely to follow the example of people whom they like, or at least, people whom they respect. It is a common misconception that leaders need to be loved by their followers. Research suggests that we might dislike some aspects of a person: their politics, perhaps, or their personal mannerisms or their background and origin. But if we respect them for their sincerity and competence, we are more likely to fall into line with what they want us to do.

LEADING IN NATIONAL CULTURES

The psychologist Geert Hofstede once referred to national culture as the 'software of the mind'. We are heavily influenced by the national cultures into which we are born, where we are educated, and where we build friendships and relationships.

As well as the obvious things like patriotism and a sense of identity, national culture also has a powerful influence through things like how we are educated. For example, university systems may vary from country to country in terms of their approaches to learning: a liberal arts approach might emphasise breadth of learning and rounded character; an analytical system based on Cartesian thinking might focus on analysis and problem solving; other systems might prioritise the absorption of facts and data. All three of these approaches will colour the thinking of university-educated leaders and followers.

Hofstede is best known for his pioneering studies of culture at computer maker IBM in the 1970s and 1980s, based on surveys of tens of thousands of employees across scores of countries. Hofstede's initial research proposition was that organisation culture would be a stronger influence than national culture. At IBM, it was widely believed that the organisation had one culture in which all employees shared, and that national cultural influences had been left behind when they joined the organisation. Hofstede wanted to demonstrate this.

However, his research found the exact opposite: that national culture had a far greater influence and that strong national cultural differences could be found across the organisation. His research has been updated frequently, and has also been developed and expanded upon by other research programmes such as Project GLOBE. The original Hofstede model has also been criticised by other scholars, usually for not going far enough in terms of identifying cultural dimensions. For example, one study of cultural differences between Canada and China found that young people in each country had more in common with their counterparts in the other country than they did with older generations in their own country.

Nevertheless, the Hofstede model has considerable explanatory power and is useful for leaders in identifying where cultural differences lie and how leaders should respond to them. His original research suggested four dimensions along which national culture could be assessed. Other dimensions were subsequently added, but we will stick with the original four for simplicity's sake. (The data for each country are available on the Hofstede project website, which at time of writing is https://geerthofstede.com/.)

Power distance

Power distance refers to how power is distributed within a society. The argument is that different societies have different power structures depending on how power is concentrated or dispersed. According to Hofstede, in societies with a high power distance score, power is strongly concentrated in the hands of a few. In government, for example, power would be concentrated in the hands of the president or monarch and their cabinet and everyone else would be expected to obey their wishes. These societies tend to be very hierarchical and formal, and people know their place in the hierarchy and conform to it. In contrast, societies with low power distance scores tend to be less hierarchical and relations between leaders and followers are less formal.

It was also assumed that people in high power distance cultures accept their situation and are happy to live with it. They want a strong hierarchy to support them; knowing their place makes people comfortable, whereas not knowing where they stand in the hierarchy can induce uncertainty and fear. However, this is approach can easily be challenged. Other research has shown that once power begins to weaken, those at the bottom of the hierarchy are quick to reject their position and attempt to seize more power for themselves and reduce the power distance. In Central and South America there is a tradition known as *caudillismo* which favours strong, often dictatorial leaders, but these leaders gain followers because they bring (temporary) stability, not simply because they are powerful. Once their power begins to weaken, followers usually rise up and overthrow them.

Individualism/collectivism

This dimension is a spectrum. At one end is individualism, where individuals are seen as important and valued for who they are and the rights of the individual take precedence over the needs of the group. Canada, with a relatively small population in a very large space, is usually seen as a quite individualist country where there is an emphasis on self-reliance and entrepreneurialism. At the other end is collectivism, where the opposite takes place: people live in close proximity to each other and rely on each other for support, with the result that the needs of the group take priority over the needs of the individual. Hofstede's method suggests that Thailand is a strongly collectivist country. Many countries are somewhere in the middle on this spectrum, meaning their cultures exhibit symptoms of both individualism *and* collectivism.

THE PARADOX OF INDIVIDUALISM AND COLLECTIVISM

The reason why many countries are in the middle of the spectrum is because of a paradox of human nature. Most individuals are capable of being both individualist and collectivist in outlook at the same time. We exist, psychologists tell us, in a constant state of tension, wanting to be free of interference from other people so we can do whatever we want, but at the same time knowing that we need other people. This is not just a matter of survival; as a species we are social animals and for most people again, the company of others is essential to mental health and well-being. The paradox within our natures translates into a larger paradox within our societies.

Uncertainty avoidance

This is effectively a measure of risk tolerance within a society. Some societies will see risk as something to be avoided, perhaps because failure is a source of shame and stigma. In others failure is seen as an acceptable (within limits), meaning that people feel they can take risks with less potential cost to themselves. The Hofstede data suggests that Japanese society is highly risk averse, while Nigeria and Norway, for various reasons, have a higher tolerance for risk.

There are of course many different kinds of risk, and a single culture might not view each kind of risk in the same way. In societies with a high level of risk avoidance, the most important risks are those that affect the person or reputation, and will impact on both their own self-esteem and their standing in society. Risks affecting money or property might be seen as more acceptable.

'Masculine'/'feminine'

This is the most controversial of Hofstede's dimensions, in large part because of the anachronistic terminology used. What Hofstede was describing here had nothing to do with gender. A 'masculine' culture in his words is one that prioritises success and achievement. Wealth, property and position in society are the visual signs of success. A 'feminine' culture, by contrast, is one where personal growth and development, well-being and happiness are prioritised over target-setting and goals. Despite their close proximity, the Hofstede data suggest that Japan is a highly achievement-oriented culture, while South Korea is a much more person-oriented culture.

Despite the controversy, this dimension is important as the connection to motivation is clear and direct. In terms of work, this dimension explains why people work: do they live to work, or do they work to live? That will affect their attitudes in the workplace, and what expectations they have of their leaders.

Implications of the Hofstede model for leadership

Of course these models are built on huge generalisations. Within any society there will be a lot of variations. We can find determined individualists in Thailand, and Canadians who believe in service to their community. There are many risk-takers and entrepreneurs in Japan, and many risk-averse Norwegians. What the study tells us, though, is important in terms of cultural expectations. While there are indeed many entrepreneurs in Japan, they have not always enjoyed much social status and are sometimes seen as outsiders. The traditional route for a young person after education was to join an established company and work for it until they retired, which was seen as much less risky than the perils of entrepreneurship or self-employment.

In a multinational organisation like IBM, or non-governmental organisations like the World Health Organization or aid charities, leading across the organisation means dealing with a wide range of cultures and cultural expectations. A leader might visit many different countries within the course of a year, or a month, and have to adapt to the different cultures of each. Or moving jobs from one company to another might also entail transfer to a different country. Police forces and armed forces often collaborate with their colleagues from other countries and leaders need to work with other leaders who perhaps have different cultures and values from their own. Top-level sports teams play in different countries, and so on.

National culture gives us a wider context and tells us what we might be faced with and what we need to be aware of. It does not provide predictive certainty, because not everyone from a culture will be the same, but it does give us parameters. Here are some of the things leaders will need to consider when thinking about each of the cultural dimensions and their own adaptive capacity:

Power distance: if power distance appears to be high, with strong hierarchies and people preferring to wait for orders rather than take responsibility, first test how genuine this is. Try giving limited responsibility to a few people, showing them first that they will not be punished if they fail, and see how they react. If this does not work, you may have to adjust your own leadership style (see next chapter) to be more directive and give people clear and precise directions. As time passes, they may become more used to you and more willing to take responsibility.

If power distance is low, with people less willing to take direct orders and preferring more responsibility, you may need to let go a little more. Distribute power and give other leaders a chance to step up, supporting them and monitoring progress.

Individualism/collectivism: if the national culture is more collectivist, this can have advantages when it comes to things like team working. People may be more used to working together and more willing to work towards a common end. However, if collectivism is combined with a high power distance, the team may also require direction. Once they know what is expected of them they will work happily together, but they will need a push to get started.

If the culture is more individualist, you may have to work harder to get people together in teams. It might be easier to try to find individual tasks that people can perform and turn them loose on these. Individualists may be happier working from home, for example, whereas collectivists will want the security of the group and would rather come into the office. As leader, you need to judge the culture of the organisation and find the right recipe.

Individualism combined with low power distance could be problematic. You might find you have a lot of ambitious self-starters who will take responsibility for their tasks and get on with the work in their own way. You might also find that they each have different ideas about what they want to do and will go off in different directions. In this combination, giving your followers orders and directions will not work. Demonstrating values and purpose and influencing the followers to coalesce around these probably offers the best chance of success.

Uncertainty avoidance: if the national culture is averse to risk and tries to avoid uncertainty, it is important for the leader to provide reassurance. Maintain continuity in terms of communications and be there as a presence for your team to rely on if they become nervous or worried. You might have to become the umbrella we referred to in Chapter 1, and try to give your team a degree of protection from what is going on around them. Your role is to reassure them and give them confidence.

If the culture is comfortable with uncertainty and risk, however, you might again need to step back and let them get on with it. Be prepared for the fact that there will be failures, and set conditions so that you and the entire organisation can learn from those failures. As leader you will also need to set boundaries: what risks are acceptable, as sources of learning and a necessary part of the innovation process, and what risks could endanger the entire organisation or cause harm to people, and will be off limits.

'Masculine'/'feminine': here you will need to consider what motivates your people. In an achievement-oriented culture, you will need to set reward structures to provide tangibles such as pay and promotion but also, importantly, recognition for what has been achieved. In a person-oriented culture, rewards will be more personal to the individual. Recognition again is important but so are personal growth, development, new skills and a sense of meaning and purpose.

LEADING IN DIFFERENT SECTOR CULTURES

Much of the literature on leadership and culture has focused on either national culture or the culture of individual organisations, and comparison of sectors has received less attention. Cultural differences between sectors are certainly visible. The armed forces are certainly different from the public sector, as we saw above, and officers from the armed forces sometimes struggle to find their feet in commercial businesses as well.

In professional services firms like accounting and consulting, factors like prestige and personal reputation, expertise and knowledge are important ingredients of the culture: these qualities are attributes expected of a leader, and are things that followers aspire to. Financial services are more used to rapid change than manufacturing. Private companies tend to be more person-centred and collectivist than public sector organisations like government departments, where power distance is higher, individual ambition is sometimes more important than collective need and status is more important than well-being. These too of course are generalisations and there are plenty of exceptions to all of these cases.

Particularly when moving from different sectors, leaders will need to look at the drivers and pressures within those sectors. Culture forms in part as a response to pressure and need. Why, for example, are financial services firms more used to rapid change? Because financial markets change from second to second, and people need to be able react to sudden, unplanned changes. They also pay more attention to forecasting the future as closely as possible, in order to put themselves into the best position to anticipate those changes. This affects the culture of these organisations from top to bottom. The main function of most manufacturing firms, on the other hand, is to produce the same products and goods, of identical quality, over and over for thousands of times. They thrive on efficient routine, which means that change does not come easily to their cultures.

Finally, we need to consider how other cultures will impact on sector culture. The culture of the financial services sector also tends to have a higher tolerance for risk: when banks make loans, for example, they know that a certain portion of those loans will never be repaid, and this is a risk that must be accepted. However, in Malaysia, Pakistan and some other countries, Islamic banks do not lend money at interest, as this is prohibited by Islamic law. Instead, they use other routes such as investing directly in the business and taking a stake in its ownership. This means they are more cautious about investments as they could potentially lose much more than they would if a loan was defaulted, and so risk avoidance is much higher.

The relationships between national culture and sector culture have far too many permutations to list here. The general principle for leaders is that the culture of their own sector may be malleable and changeable, and will take different forms in different countries and regions. Don't assume that the same attitudes to power distance or risk will prevail in your sector everywhere in the world. Bank managers in the USA may be heavily motivated by personal reward and the chance for promotion, but in China they will probably be more motivated by service to their own organisation, meaning they will have different expectations of leadership. The leadership space has multiple cultural dimensions, and these need to be recognised and understood.

LEADING IN DIFFERENT ORGANISATIONAL CULTURES

Within sectors there will often be large variations in culture *between* organisations, even ones that appear to be quite similar. There will also be cultural variations *within* organisations, leading to sub-cultures and different behaviours and expectations, even in organisations that operate only in one sector and one country. There are currently forty-three police forces in the UK, each with exactly the same role and mission, but there are distinct cultural variations between them. What is more, there are also differences between different elements in each force: between uniformed officers and civilian staff, and between ordinary front-line officers and armed response teams, to take just two examples. These variations can sometimes lead to misunderstandings and clashes of values.

Some of the factors leading to these variations include:

- *Size.* Because large organisations are more complex, they necessarily have more structure and hierarchy. Herbert Simon, the social scientist who wrote about complexity in the 1950s, identified hierarchy as an important component of complex systems because it allows each element of the system to know where it fits in and what its role is. Cultures in large organisations will have more internal variations and sub-culture. By contrast, smaller organisations will have simpler structures with less room for cultural variations.
- *Age.* Culture takes time to develop. The cultures or recently established organisations are likely to be heavily influenced by purpose and process; a start-up tech firm's culture will likely revolve around the technology the company is developing and its purpose and uses. The Church of England, which was established in the early sixteenth century, has had four hundred years to develop, and consequently has far more symbols and traditions and beliefs embedded in its culture. Leaders often find these old, entrenched cultures very hard to shift.
- *Function.* What the organisation does will influence its culture. The differences in culture between, say, the armed forces and the Church of England are obvious: one is committed to peace, the other is trained for war. We touched on this element already in the discussion of sector cultures, but the influence of function is also strongly present in the sub-cultures within organisations. We mentioned the police above, but consider also the army, which has distinctions between infantry, artillery, engineers, supply and logistics, communications specialists, drone operators and many others. In corporations we see cultural differences between operations, marketing, finance, human resources and other functions: operations might be

focused on precision and process, marketing will be all about relationships, finance focuses on data and accountability and so on, all of which lead to different outlooks and mindsets. Leaders need to be able to understand all of these cultures and manage across them.

- *Purpose.* As well as function, the purpose the organisation has set for itself will also influence culture. Non-governmental organisations established to alleviate poverty or provide aid to refugees will perceive value and purpose differently from banks or manufacturing companies. Each will attract different kinds of people, whose personal values will help to create and reinforce the culture.
- *Leadership.* As we said, it is doubtful whether leaders can control culture but they can certainly influence it. How well they do so depends in part on their own competence and their own sense of values and purpose. Leaders with a strong sense of ethics and a clear vision will try to influence a culture in a positive way, focusing it on the common mission. As we shall see in Chapter 8, though, incompetent leadership or toxic leadership can have a destructive effect on culture.
- *People.* The people who join the organisation are an important variable. Their backgrounds, beliefs and experiences will differ, and the combination of these elements feeds into the organisation's culture.

The combination of these and other factors will be different every time, and this is the reason why each organisation's culture will be distinctive and unique. Leaders need to analyse each culture in order to understand it and know what leadership style and role will be best suited to that culture (see Chapter 6). There are a number of frameworks for analysing culture, but here we have chosen two that have stood the test of time.

The first comes from the work of psychologist Edgar Schein, credited by some with founding the discipline of organisation behaviour. Schein analysed organisation cultures on three levels:

- *Artefacts and behaviours. Artefacts* are the physical evidence of a culture. They can include things like the layout of an office or manufacturing facility or workshop, dress codes and uniforms, signs and symbols. We saw earlier how companies like Tata and McKinsey display symbols that remind people of the corporate values. Military units and police forces have badges and uniforms, and cities and countries will have flags and coats of arms. All of these artefacts serve to remind people of the culture.

Behaviours include formal documents like codes of conduct and codes of ethics, but also informal things like how people communicate, the degree of formality they have with each other (do people call each other by their first name, or are titles used?) and the stories and joke they tell each other. Sometimes artefacts and behaviours are combined in ceremonies or rituals. Some Japanese firms still start each working day with employees standing in front of the company flag and singing the company song.

- *Espoused values.* Codes of conduct and codes of ethics are also part of what Schein calls 'espoused values', the things the company believes in: in other words, its values and purpose. 'Espoused' in this case means the values that are stated publicly, but this brings an interesting point; are the publicly stated values the real ones? The UK utility company Thames Water has a statement of commitment to a clean environment on its website, indicating that this commitment is part of its values, but according to media report, the company pumped more than seventy billion litres of untreated sewage into rivers from 2020 to 2025. What does this say about the company's real values?
- *Assumptions.* This term refers to deeply ingrained habits and understandings and views of the world that are common to most members of the organisation. Some assumptions are connected to team's purpose; for example, in team sports there is an assumption that everyone will give their utmost effort to helping the team win. In other cases the assumption might be about the workplace or working conditions; for example, people might assume that they will always be paid on time. Other assumptions concern things in the environment that could affect work, including superstitions: in the United States Navy it is considered unlucky for a ship to leave

port and set to sea on a Friday, and the navy still tries to avoid doing so if possible.

Schein's three layers are helpful in understanding how people perceive their own culture. Another writer on organisations, Charles Handy, classified cultures according to what each culture deems to be most important, as follows:

- *Power culture.* Power is concentrated in the hands of a few people at the top or centre of the organisation, and the rest of the organisation is expected to be subservient to them. Followers should obey their leaders and not challenge them. All key decisions are made by the senior leaders. This is the equivalent of Hofstede's high power distance, which similarly describes a concentration of power in the hands of a few. An individual's importance in this culture is determined by how much power they have.
- *Task culture.* Task cultures are the opposite, distributing power to small teams who take responsibility for their own work. Experts who have particularly important skills will play key roles, and others will work to support them. Task cultures are particularly suited to organisations where there is a lot of project work and people need the ability to respond quickly to new situations. An individual's importance in this culture is determined by how much they know and what skills they have.
- *Role culture.* Role cultures are strongly hierarchical and bureaucratic. They put a lot of emphasis on standardised processes, controls, reporting and monitoring. Independent action is discouraged, and permission always has to be obtained by someone further up the chain of command. An individual's importance in this culture is determined by their job title and where they stand in terms of seniority.
- *Person culture.* The person culture focuses on the individuals in the organisation and sees service to members as the purpose of the organisation. While members put into the organisation, it is expected that they will also gain a great deal of benefit in terms of personal development, good health, etc. Gyms

and sports clubs are examples. All individuals are considered equally important in this culture.

Handy emphasises the point that no organisation has just one of these types of culture, and indeed, most organisations will probably have elements of all four. A corporation, for example might give responsibility for the most important decisions to the board of directors (power culture) but distribute power and give responsibility for tasks to individual teams (task culture), using an established hierarchy for transmitting information (role culture) but ensuring that people have development opportunities and looking after their well-being (person culture). An army unit would have a commanding officer (power culture) supported by other subordinate officers (role culture) with the unit trained to fight in certain ways (task culture) but with support given to the soldiers and their families to ensure that they are looked after (person culture).

What differs, says Handy, is the balance between elements. Take two rival corporations. One might be an old established firm where power culture and role culture are dominant: decisions are made through a hierarchy with power concentrated at the top. Another, newer firm might not have had time to build strong structures. Here the focus is on getting things done, and teams play a vital role. The emphasis would be on task culture, with person culture in a supporting position. The important point is to ensure that the right balance of all four is present, and part of the task of leadership is to change the balance if necessary. If there is too much emphasis on hierarchy and roles, consider breaking the organisation into teams as we saw in the department store example earlier. If the teams lack direction, it might necessary to tilt the balance a bit more towards the power culture, giving more direction from the centre.

Now, let us consider the implications of Handy's model for Schein's three levels, and what each level looks like with each culture. Bearing in mind the point just made that elements of all four cultures will be present, we need to look at all of these levels and see what each looks like in the context of the organisation. Remember, too, that each culture is unique so what these elements look like will always be different in practice.

Table 5.1 Schein's layers mapped onto Handy's model

Power culture	*Artefacts and behaviours*	Workplaces will be formal settings with reminders of where power lies: corner offices, reserved parking spaces for top managers, etc. Senior leaders will be treated with respect, though behaviour may be less formal among followers.
	Espoused values	A range of values may be present, but there is likely to be a focus on issues like preserving the organisation, defending it against competition and so on. Senior leaders may see themselves as stewards of the organisation, dedicated to preserving it; alternatively, they may use their power to exploit others and serve their own ends.
	Assumptions	Hierarchy is to be respected. Duty is a virtue, and people are rewarded for how well they do their duty. Instructions, once received, must always be obeyed.
Task culture	*Artefacts and behaviours*	Workplaces will often be informal, with lots of open spaces for team working. There is less hierarchy of space; even senior leaders may have small offices or hot desks. Senior leaders dress casually and are often indistinguishable from followers. People often call each other by their first names.
	Espoused values	Value creation is important but so is efficient team working. At best, the values focus on getting the job done and creating value for stakeholders. At worst, the group can self-identify too strongly and descend into groupthink.
	Assumptions	Teams are the most valuable part of the organisation because they are where value is created. Teamworking is something that everyone is expected to be good at. Communications from senior leaders will be more open and phrased as goals and statements of direction rather than detailed instructions.

(*Continued*)

Table 5.1 (Continued)

Role culture	*Artefacts and behaviours*	Workplaces will be formal with visible signs of rank and hierarchy such as uniforms and badges of rank. People will often address each other by rank or title, especially if they are not part of the same team or group.
	Espoused values	Hierarchy is seen as a good thing in and of itself. Duty is not so much to the organisation and its stakeholders as to preserving the hierarchy and the existing order. Change is distrusted, and stability is a key goal.
	Assumptions	Nothing should change without good reason, and probably not even then. Authority and orders should not be questioned. In the worst cases, orders are often not made clear; people are expected to understand what is needed of them and perform without asking questions. On the other end of the spectrum, the hierarchy exists to facilitate communications and transmit information, like the fire control system we discussed in Chapter 4.
Person culture	*Artefacts and behaviours*	Workplaces will be highly personalised with lots of photos, plants and other personal artefacts. Communication is informal. Hierarchies are weak and leaders, where present, are indistinguishable from followers. In some cases this openness extends to outsiders, who are made welcome and treated as part of the group, but this does not always happen.
	Espoused values	People matter. Human development is a core value and the organisation exists to serve its people. There is a danger that an in-group could take over and the organisation could exclude or even punish outsiders, while remaining supportive of the people on the inside.
	Assumptions	People will be kind and supportive and will work to help each other. If anyone needs help from the wider organisation, that help will always be provided. Followers will get more out of their work than they put in.

This is only a partial picture, of course. As noted, any organisation is likely to be a patchwork of all of these cultural features and many more. For leadership, the challenge is to interpret the signs we see, the behaviours of our people and the symbols they respect, and work out what they mean and what lies behind them. Only then can we hope to influence culture in any effective way.

LEADERSHIP ACROSS TIME

We have already discussed some of the impacts of change, but we need to go into the subject in a bit more detail. As Heraclitus of Ephesos noted, change is omnipresent, and leaders have to be constantly aware of how their own situation is changing and how they themselves need to change and evolve as well. Change happens at multiple levels, and often at different speeds:

- The environment changes.
- The organisation changes.
- The people change.
- We change.

THE PARADOX OF CHANGE AND STABILITY

Human beings are conditioned to seek stability. Our brains tell us that stability is safe; we know where we are and we understand our environment, and this makes us happy. Change represents uncertainty: we don't know what is coming next, and that makes us fearful. This applies to leaders as well as followers.

Logically, we know we must change; instinctively, we seek stability. This paradox leads to many seemingly eccentric forms of behaviour, such as people refusing to leave their homes even though they are on the edge of a volcano about to erupt. A branch of psychology known as terror management theory talks about the lengths we will go to convince ourselves that dangerous situations are actually quite safe. We are caught in continuous trap whereby we try to both change and seek stability at the same time.

The environment changes

Environmental changes can be big and powerful forces like climate change, war, pandemics or the sudden appearance of new technologies. Or they can be smaller and subtler, harder to detect, like changes in consumer confidence or preferences, or the changing expectations of society. Different generations have different expectations of work and life. Baby boomers believed in hard work and the importance of property, and often lived to work. Gen Z is less certain about property; many have given up on the idea of ever being able to afford a home. They are more likely to work to live.

As leaders, we cannot control environmental forces. We can only observe them, anticipate them and try to meet them. That is one of a leader's core tasks. Followers are usually concentrated on their own tasks and often don't have time to study the world around them. Leaders can step back and look at the wider picture. However, we need to remember the paradox of now and then from Chapter 4, and not get so preoccupied with the future that we neglect the present.

The organisation changes

Changes within organisations, on the other hand, are something that leaders can influence, if not entirely control (see Chapter 2). Leaders need to be aware of change across four dimensions: *culture*, *strategy*, *structure* and *process*.

LEADERSHIP AND CULTURE CHANGE

We have already discussed culture in quite a lot of detail, but from a leadership perspective there is one more point to be made: culture is dynamic. External pressures, internal dynamics, changes in the composition of teams, relationship breakdowns and emotional crises, the actions of leaders themselves can all impact on the culture. To repeat the earlier point, culture is powerful but culture is also fragile. A lot of leadership time is spent trying to build and maintain a strong culture through influence, and the process is continuous throughout the life of the organisation. There is never a point where a leader can say, 'we now have the perfect culture', and stop. Tomorrow, the dynamics will have changed and the process of influencing starts all over again.

LEADERSHIP AND STRATEGIC CHANGE

Strategy is the roadmap the organisation uses to reach its goals. It is generally described as falling into two parts, making strategy and implementing strategy, although the Japanese strategy guru Kenichi Ohmae argued that the two things should happen at the same time. Making strategy and guiding its implementation are among the most important tasks of the leader.

Making strategy would be easy if everything stayed the same. Unlike a roadmap, however, strategic plans have to take account of a constantly shifting and changing environment. Here is where the leader's ability to see the bigger picture comes in. The leader looks around them, anticipating change and crafting strategy in response.

However, that process will always be imperfect, because in the course implementing the strategy and moving towards the goal, *more* things will happen that threaten to derail the strategy and bring it to a halt. Helmuth von Moltke, the nineteenth-century Prussian general, once wrote that 'no plan survives contact with the enemy', meaning that rivals and competitors will always behave in unexpected ways. We could abbreviate Moltke's statement to simply: 'no plan survives'. All plans need to be flexible enough to allow for a change of course to deal with the unexpected, and it is the leader's responsibility to see that this is done.

This is where complexity comes back into the picture. Rather than concentrating on just one issue at a time, as leaders we need to look at the whole picture and search for patterns. Strategy itself is complex, or should be: a large number of variables have to be accounted for. Leaders need to identify those variables and build them into their planning.

THE PARADOX OF PROACTIVE AND REACTIVE

As leaders we need to simultaneously be proactive, scanning the environment for threats and opportunities, devising responses, bringing in people and resources to take advantage of opportunities. But we also have to be reactive, looking for threats that might emerge from nowhere. We have to do both of these things simultaneously. If we are only proactive, we will be caught unprepared when threats emerge. If we are only reactive, we will be unable to seize opportunities when they arise, and someone else will step in and take advantage instead.

LEADERSHIP AND STRUCTURAL CHANGE

In theory, changing the structure of an organisation is one of the easiest parts of leadership. All a leader has to do, or so it is said, is redesign the structure to make it simpler and/or more efficient and focused. Merge a couple of teams here, get rid of another team that is no longer necessary, and the job is done.

In practice, most restructurings don't work very well because leaders don't get the basics right. Restructuring means change, and as we saw earlier, most change makes people nervous. The first step in any restructuring is to make it very clear to everyone involved what will happen and how it will affect them, hopefully in a positive way. Restructuring also needs to be thought through in terms of the impact on processes and communications. Will simplifying the organisation improve people's ability to communicate, or make it worse? Once again, organisations need to be thought of as complex systems. Each element of the system needs to be analysed in terms of not only its own functionality but how it connects with the wider system. The point to remember is that structure is not just a collection of random parts. Like Lego bricks or a jigsaw puzzle, every piece needs to slot into place.

LEADERSHIP AND PROCESS CHANGE

One of the arts of process change for a leader is knowing when to change a process and when to leave it alone. In many organisations there is a lot of unnecessary process change, for example, upgrading to the latest version of software regardless of whether this will result in any real process improvements.

Generally speaking, the followers who actually use the processes will know more about that process than the leadership, so it could be argued that they are the ones to decide when processes need to be upgraded or changed. The countervailing view is that, because most people don't like change, followers will cling to the old ways of doing things long after they should have let go. Leaders can contribute by learning about the potential of new processes and new technologies and then discussing these with their teams. The decision about when and what to change should be a mutual one.

The people change

It may seem an obvious point, but the composition of any organisation will change over time. People come and go. Personal circumstances and family life change meaning. People grow bored and move on, searching for new opportunities. Some become stressed and burned out, or reach retirement age. When they depart, others come to replace them. As the organisation grows, more people are brought in.

Change and flux in the composition of organisations are a constant, and the larger the organisation, the more frequent these changes will be. In a large organisation, people will depart and new recruits will be hired every day, meaning that senior leaders at the top of the organisation don't even know for certain how many people they employ.

For leaders, the task of managing team composition is never done. It is important to recognise this, and to see it as a positive. Think about what would happen if the people *didn't* come and go. The same people would remain in the same jobs, year after year. That might make it easier to get to know them and lead them, but the people themselves would suffer. There would be no opportunities for promotion and advancement or to move to different jobs or occupations. Boredom would set in, motivation levels would decline and followers would become less creative and less productive. Organisations bring in new people with new ideas in order to avoid becoming stale.

Even when they remain in post, people still change and evolve. Younger employees are often more motivated by pay but also by the comradeship and teamship of being part of an organisation. Older employees may be more thoughtful and increasingly search for meaning in their work. Or the opposite may be true: younger followers might be idealists wanting to do something meaningful to them, while older people are coasting towards retirement.

Leaders need to monitor the people in their teams and know where they are in their life journey. For leaders at the top, this means being mindful of the people around them; and also, encouraging them to do the same for their own followers, and so on through the hierarchy. This reminds us again that leadership is a process that takes place in a space between leaders and followers. Leaders cannot prevent followers from leaving, and they have no control whatever over how people and their motivations change over time. Leadership can only be a partnership between leaders and followers.

We change

Just like our followers, we also change with time. We learn from our own successes and those of others around us; we also fail from time to time, and while hopefully we learn from that too, failures can damage confidence and leave mental scars. We form relationships and attachments; we may start families or take on other caring responsibilities. We lose friends and family members too, and endure grief. All of these things change us mentally and emotionally.

As leaders, we do not close the door on these things when we reach the office. They are part of us, and it is foolish and dangerous to try to suppress them. Leaders that do try to detach their working lives from their personal life often end up by burning out or suffering mental health problems.

We hope that over time we will get better at leading, and that lessons we learned in the past will stay with us and we will become more effective, more compassionate, more empathetic, more trustworthy and more knowledgeable. We must remain alive to the danger, however, that we have not learned and that we might indeed be changing for the worse. Earlier we mentioned the Dunning-Kruger effect, the myth of illusory superiority that sometimes comes with success. We listen to other people's praise and begin to believe that we really are superior to others.

This is dangerous because it risks detaching leaders from reality. Research suggests that while the majority of leaders see themselves in a positive light, the percentage of their followers who view them positively is far less. It is easy for a leader to convince themselves that their followers trust and respect them, because admitting otherwise would be a blow to that leader's self-esteem. Followers may also pretend to respect the leader because they fear retribution if they do otherwise. In reality, trust has been broken and followers are angry, resentful and preparing to either resist or leave the organisation entirely.

Reflection and self-awareness are essential components of leadership. As leaders, we simply *must* look critically at ourselves and reflect on our own performance objectively. Others can assist us with this: mentors and critical friends are very useful for helping us to see ourselves as others see us.

HENRY FORD

The first part of Henry Ford's career looks like the ultimate success story. An engineer and racing driver, Ford set up the Ford Motor Company in 1903, and co-designed one of the most iconic cars of all times, the Model T, which launched in 1908. But Ford was more than just a talented designer. He built a state-of-the-art production facility at Highland Park, near Detroit in the state of Michigan, which revolutionised car building. Hitherto cars had been built by hand by teams of workers in a workshop. Ford adapted the concepts of interchangeable parts and the assembly line in a way that produced cars quickly and cheaply. Over the next twenty years, more than seventeen million Model Ts were sold all around the world.

Of course Ford did not do this all on his own. His own team of senior managers, William Knudsen, James Couzens and Charles Sorenson, has been described as one of the best management teams the world has seen. Ford also recruited the best workers. He paid his people five dollars a day, at a time when the going rate in the automobile industry was about one dollar per day, meaning that he could take his pick of the best and most skilled workers. He treated his workers well and won their respect both for his knowledge of the industry and for his fairness and values. In his writings at the time Ford often referred to the importance of recruiting good workers and treating them well, and also reiterated his belief that the first duty of any business was to be of service to the people.

But Ford changed over time. People called him the greatest man in the world, and he began to believe it. He became arrogant and overbearing. He drove his best leaders, Knudsen and Couzens, out of the business and tried to gather more and more control into his own hands. Trying to manage such a vast company inevitably led to failures. The Model A, successor to the Model T, was a good car but failed in the market. A venture to set up a production facility in Brazil to make rubber for car tyres failed with heavy losses. Ford did not take responsibility for these, but blamed other people.

By the 1930s Ford had become a tyrant. Wages were cut and working conditions deteriorated. When workers protested and tried to form unions, Ford turned to the local mafia for help and hired thugs to beat up the workers. Even his son Edsel, whom he had appointed at his successor, was bullied and abused. Rival companies like General Motors overtook Ford in the market and by the late 1940s the company was on the edge of bankruptcy. Finally, Ford's wife and grandson threatened to sell their shares in the company to rivals unless he stepped down, and Ford was forced to resign.

Opinions vary as to what changed in Ford. He certainly seems to have believed in his own greatness and thought he could never fail. Megalomania was present, but there seem to have been other forms of mental illness as well. But most importantly, there were no checks and balances at the Ford Motor Company. The lack of effective governance meant that there was nothing to prevent Ford from doing whatever he wanted. Trust between followers and leaders, which had once been one of the company's great strengths, was broken. And crucially, Ford had no mentors or critical friends who might have been able to help him reflect and understand what was really happening. Ultimately, Ford's career is a cautionary tale, reminding us that even the best and most idealistic leaders can go wrong.

LEADERSHIP ACROSS SPACE

By 'space' we mean here not only physical space but also the situation in which the organisation and its leaders find themselves. *Situation* can be understood as a combination of place and time.

PHYSICAL SPACE

The span of control, which we discussed in Chapter 2, has clear spatial implications. 'Controlling' a team is easier when team members are in close proximity and can see and hear each other whenever required. When they are more widely dispersed, working in virtual teams and dispersed around the globe, the problems of control and coordination can become much harder.

This is not universal, however, and many dispersed teams do function very well. The myth that 'people are more productive in the office' ignores the fact that in many sectors people have been working in dispersed teams for decades, even before the invention of the internet. University academics collaborated on research projects, banks and investment houses did multi-national investment deals and armies coordinated the movement of troops in the field, often over vast distances.

As we saw with the span of control, coordinating across space requires leaders to train or promote other trusted leaders and put them in positions where they can exercise local control. If this cannot be done, there is a strong possibility that the local teams and followers will simply ignore direction from the top and go their own way. This has been a constant theme in military history: commanders of detached military units have interpreted orders as they thought best, got it wrong and ended up creating a disaster. In 1854 during the Crimean War the commander of the Light Brigade, Lord Cardigan, was ordered to attack a Russian artillery position. He misunderstood the order and led his cavalry to attack another much stronger position. Casualties among men and horses were so high that the Light Brigade was no longer an effective fighting force.

This highlights another need when leading across physical space: strong communications links. The link between Lord Cardigan and his commanding officer, Lord Raglan, was a single courier, Captain Nolan. When he saw that the Light Brigade was about to attack the wrong position, Nolan tried to warn Cardigan but was killed before he could speak. There was no one else available to correct the mistake. The Medici Bank, by contrast, always sent multiple copies of messages by separate couriers or ships in case one was lost along the way: the message would always get through.

Today the technology is different, but the issue remains the same. Multiple communications channels need to be established with subsidiaries in case one system fails. Leaders need to make sure these channels are in place, and be assured that everyone has been fully trained and knows how to use them.

SITUATION

Leaders need to be looking to the future and trying to anticipate what will come next, but they also need to focus on what is happening right here and now. Can the organisation cope with the pressures it is under, or does the leader need to intervene? If the latter, what form should that intervention take?

As always there is a broad spectrum of possibilities here, but let us try to look at some basic principles. At any given time, two forces will be at work:

- *External pressures*, which can span a wide range of forces: competition in business, climate change and natural disaster, geopolitical forces, wider economic trends, changing social needs and many others.
- *Capability for response*, which depends to a large extent on the skills and experience of followers and their ability to work together.

This simple classification masks a huge range of issues that leaders need to be thinking about at any given moment, but to help narrow down the options a little we can classify each of these forces as high or low. That gives us as leaders an idea of what range of responses we should be considering. For ease of analysis, we have divided the types of response into four classifications: *preparation*, *observation*, and *participation*.

Let us look at each of these in a little more detail.

- *Preparation*: the team is not under a great deal of pressure at the moment and is working smoothly, but that situation may not last. Followers lack experience and the organisation is vulnerable if a sudden threat should arrive: the appearance of a new

Table 5.2 Pressure and capability

	Low external pressure	*High external pressure*
Low capability for response	Preparation	Intervention
High capability for response	Observation	Participation

technology like AI, an enemy attack, a natural disaster. Now is the time for training and practice, to improve skills and make the organisation more robust for the future.

- *Observation*: pressure is not especially high and the team are skilled and experienced, and well able to handle whatever is coming their way. If the leader gets too involved now, it could look like micromanagement. This is a time for leaders to step back, observe what is happening, offer encouragement and motivation, but be prepared to step in should things change.
- *Intervention*: the organisation is under a lot of pressure and people are struggling. Nothing in their experience or skills has prepared them for what is happening now. The leader needs to get involved, using their own skills and knowledge to help followers solve problems. Influence is also needed to motivate followers and give them the confidence to face the situation. Once the crisis is past, the leader can step back again.
- *Participation*: the pressure is high but the organisation is dealing with the strain. Even though they are coping with the situation, people will still be looking to their leaders for reassurance. The leader needs to be present, and will create more trust and respect if they show themselves willing to get involved. The key question for the leader to be asking here is, 'how can I help you?'

This is a fairly crude generalisation, but it does show us how we as leaders can recognise situations and craft our own response. It should be noted that there are other similar frameworks that can be used as well. For example, Paul Hersey and Ken Blanchard in their work on situational leadership categorised organisations according to ability and willingness and identified four leadership styles: directing, coaching, supporting and delegating.

This has necessarily been a long chapter, because *all* leadership is affected by culture, time and space. These factors determine how we should respond and what roles we should play, and that is the subject of the next chapter.

FURTHER READING

Handy, C., *Understanding Organizations*, Penguin, 1993.

Hersey, P., *The Situational Leader*, Prentice-Hall, 1986.

Hofstede, G., *Culture's Consequences: Comparing Values, Behaviors, Institutions and Organizations Across Nations*, Sage, 2003.

Knights, D. and Willmott, H., *Introducing Organizational Behaviour and Management*, Cengage Learning, 2012.

Ohmae, K., *The Mind of the Strategist: The Art of Japanese Business*, McGraw-Hill, 1991.

Schein, E.H., *Organizational Culture and Leadership*, Jossey-Bass, 2016.

Simon, H.A., *The Sciences of the Artificial*, MIT Press, 1996.

6

ROLES AND AUTHENTICITY IN LEADERSHIP

We have established that leadership is a process that happens in the space between leaders and followers, and that effective leadership depends on the relationship between the two. Ideally, the leadership process should be a partnership between leaders and followers. We should be seeing them as two halves of the same whole, rather than separate parties or – even worse – adversaries.

Both leaders and followers will seek to influence each other. How well leaders succeed depends on the perceptions other have of them. Are they trustworthy? Are they fair? Are they compassionate? Are they someone that we, as followers, can relate to?

Two bodies of theory in leadership are important to consider here. The first is *authenticity*, which posits that leaders should behave in a manner that is true to themselves. Honesty, fairness and self-awareness are all part of this, but there is also an implication that the leader should be 'real'. The second body of theory is *role theory*, which suggests that we all play different roles at various times in our lives, and that we adapt and change roles depending on the situation we are in. There is of course a contradiction between the two.

DOI: 10.4324/9781003496243-6

THE PARADOX OF ROLES AND AUTHENTICITY

As leaders, we need to be authentic and true to ourselves, but we also have to conform to other people's expectations of us and find ways to influence them, which means that we have to find ways of adapting how we communicate and how we relate to other people. This involves the playing of roles. The challenge for leaders is to find out how to play roles in an authentic way.

This is not just a leadership problem. Followers also play roles, and have the same problems with finding out how to do so authentically.

AUTHENTICITY

The concept of authenticity has been discussed by philosophers for many centuries. Most believed that authenticity was achieved through reflection and self-awareness. Ancient Greek philosophers urged people to know themselves, while their Daoist and Buddhist counterparts in east and south Asia introduced the concept of embracing the true self. Sufism, the mystical Islamic sect, also emphasises purity of self. All of these beliefs were predicated on the notion that in the course of our lives we take on emotional and intellectual baggage: we try too hard to satisfy others, we become preoccupied with worldly things like money and property, we enter into relationships that sometimes damage us. All of these prevent us from realising the potential of our true selves.

In leadership studies, writing about authenticity initially focused on two aspects, the need for self-reflection and strong values, and the relationship between authenticity and trust. The first drew on the philosophical traditions outlined above, and suggested that by being true to ourselves we become clearer about our own purpose and will be able to identify our own values more clearly. This will make us stronger and more resilient. There is evidence that people who have clarity of purpose are also strong leaders. We can think perhaps of Nelson Mandela, who never lost sight of his own goal of bringing equality and freedom to South Africa, or

Robert the Bruce, the hero of Scottish independence who fought for nearly twenty years to drive the English out of Scotland, but these heroic examples are just the tip of the iceberg; many leaders in many fields of endeavour strive for this kind of authenticity. An Indian business leader, the late RK Krishna Kumar, told me in an interview that whenever his business faced a crisis he would 'refresh himself in the values' and emerge a stronger person, ready to carry on the fight.

Authenticity has also been linked to trust. In his book *Authentic*, Stephen Jones makes the point that people are more likely to trust a leader whom they believe to be genuine. What people say and do, he says, reflects what they think and feel, and what they think and feel is in turn a reflection of who they are (or, it could be argued, who they believe themselves to be). There is again good evidence that when leaders demonstrate their values through actions as well as words, the leaders are perceived to be more genuine and therefore more trustworthy.

The reason for this is that in our minds we equate authenticity with certainty. If a leader is playing a part, we don't know who they really are and this creates doubt in our minds. Is the leader playing this part just to make us fall into line with what they want? Can they be trusted, or are they taking advantage of us? On the other hand, if what we see is the 'real' person, we are reassured; they mean what they are telling us, and we can take them at their word.

Another quality of authenticity is accepting responsibility: authentic leaders don't try to blame others for their own mistakes; they admit their own fault and take the consequences. If the followers trust the leader, this admission of mistakes will likely strengthen that trust by providing further proof of the leader's humanity. (On the other hand, if the followers don't trust the leader, they are likely to blame them for the error, regardless of whether it was the leader's fault.) This leads us to a further point: authenticity doesn't mean the leader has to be perfect. Mistakes will always be made: in words attributed to the financier Warren Buffett, 'if you can't make mistakes, you can't make decisions.' The important thing is to manage followers' expectations and make it clear that they are allowed to make mistakes too.

Authenticity doesn't necessarily mean being 'nice' or 'good', and some authentic leaders can be quite forceful or even brutal. During his tenure as manager of the football club Manchester United, Sir Alex Ferguson became famous for his 'hairdryer' technique, which consisted of shouting at close range into the faces of players who had displeased him. Sir Georg Solti, one of the leading orchestral conductors of his day, never hesitated to use sharp language to musicians who failed to meet his demanding standards. Authenticity can have sharp edges, and sometimes playing a role which is not fully authentic is necessary to blunt some of those edges.

Nor is authenticity on its own any kind of guarantee of leadership success. One strand of authenticity theory focused on the creation of 'authenticity indices' which would supposedly enable to leaders to measure how authentic they really were. This aroused a great deal of scepticism and critique of authenticity theory more generally. Tomas Chamorro-Premuzic, for example, reminds us that leadership is situational (see Chapter 5). Authenticity, he says, does not change: if it did, it would no longer be authentic. But leaders must adapt to the situations in which they find themselves.

The point is a good one, and it highlights once again the importance of the paradox of roles and authenticity. Leaders must be capable of change and adaptation. Yet if they change too much, followers begin to doubt whether they are genuine and lose trust.

THE TRULY AUTHENTIC LEADER

Where are the truly authentic leaders?

Actually, there is no such thing as a completely authentic leader. No one is fully authentic all of the time. And if they were, they would probably be so insufferable that we would shun their company.

All leaders at some point in time fail to live up to their own values. Gerald Ratner, who had built up the world's largest chain of jewellery stores by offering quality and value, made a speech that denigrated his customers and referred to some of his products as 'crap'. He lost his company as a result. Martin Luther King, leader of the American civil rights movement, was publicly passionate about freedom and equal rights. In private, he made misogynistic comments and was reportedly unfaithful to his wife. The Duke of Wellington, who insisted that his officers be truthful and honest, ordered a painting of his famous victory at the Battle of Waterloo to be altered so as to magnify his own role and downplay the part played by his Prussian allies.

Does this matter? Was Ratner any less talented as a business leader? Should King's role in the civil rights movement be dismissed? Was Wellington any less successful as a military commander? The answer is probably no. But we need to see our leaders as human beings like us, and our leaders also need to make sure that they show us their humanity and not pretend to be superior beings. Oliver Cromwell, who ruled England as Lord Protector after the English Civil War, instructed a portrait artist to depict his face exactly as it was, 'warts and all'. Cromwell was far from perfect as a leader, but the important point here is that he knew it, and never pretended to be otherwise. Accepting him as a leader meant accepting his imperfections.

The best way of demonstrating authenticity is to be human. Don't try to be perfect or give other people unreasonable expectations of you, and accept that as Chamorro-Premuzic says, you will also have to adapt.

ROLE THEORY

Role theory starts from the premise that we adapt according to circumstances and the expectations of others around us. In doing so we play roles, not dissimilar to the roles that actors play on stage or in film. Further to this, we all play multiple roles, and we slip back and forth between them as the situation requires.

Let me use myself as an example of this. At various times in the course of the day, I am a module lead directing courses in management education, a writer working with colleagues on various projects, a friend who socialises with others, a neighbour who plays a role in the community and a husband who is in mourning for the loss of his wife to cancer. All of these situations require to behave differently. At work, I am a professional who concentrates on giving guidance and communicating to others, which requires me to be prominent and speak decisively. At home I am much quieter, often content to sit back and listen to others. In my private life I am contemplative and focus on memories; at work, I must be in the present and also consider the future.

Think about yourself and some of the roles you play in your daily life. You will probably have a family, and that itself involves multiple roles: son or daughter, spouse or partner, sibling, parent. You will have various social roles in your community. At work you may well be simultaneously a follower and a leader. Now, think about your leaders. They too are playing those same multiple roles.

HOW ROLES ARE DEFINED

Because we want instinctively to be able to control our own lives and events around us, we often assume that we define the roles we play. To an extent, we do. We make decisions, consciously or unconsciously, about which roles are appropriate at a given moment and when we need to change. At home, we are a partner and parent, but when we arrive at work we change roles and become a team leader. We believe that we are in control of this process of change.

However, research in psychology suggests otherwise. Most people want, instinctively, to be liked and respected by the people around them; few deliberately choose to be in adversarial relationships. In order to earn the liking and respect of others, we adapt our behaviour. We do not treat our staff like children and scold them when they do wrong, nor do we set performance targets for our life partners; not, that is, if we want the relationship to last.

Within the leadership space, the relationship between leaders and followers, another level of calculation is going on. Leaders are watching and listening to their followers and trying to interpret their words and body language and actions in order to find out what followers want. Simultaneously, followers are doing the same with their leaders, trying to interpret what the leader is saying, looking beneath the words for deeper meaning. Watching how their leaders speak, *their* body language, even things like how they dress, will give them clues. A leader who dresses formally in a suit and expensive shoes will send different signals to followers than one who wears jeans and a shirt with the sleeves rolled up.

As a result of these signals, we adjust the roles we play. If we are in a team with an informal culture where there is a lot of laughter and joking, we will probably join in. If we are in an organisation with a lot of hierarchy where people address each other formally, we are likely to do the same. If a leader begins laughing and joking in an organisation where there is a lot of politeness and protocol, doubt will be raised in the minds of followers about how well the leader really understands the organisation. Trust will be weakened.

This is particularly the case when a new leader arrives with a new team. Each will observe the other and interpret what they see. The problem, of course, is that these interpretations are often flawed and incorrect. Cognitive bias (which we will discuss in a moment) means that we often have preconceptions of other people, impressions that have formed in our minds even before we meet them, based on their backgrounds or what we have heard about them.

Paradoxically, the best way that a leader can avoid misperception by followers is to be authentic. Demonstrate clearly, through actions as well as words, what your values are. Earlier in the book we saw the example of Squadron Leader Bader taking command of 242 Squadron. The pilots were sceptical, having decided in their minds beforehand that he was not an effective leader. He proved them wrong, first by demonstrating technical competence and second by helping them meet their unsatisfied needs for fresh kit and good food. This changed the minds of the pilots and they began to trust Bader.

However, leaders also need to watch and listen to their followers and work out what their expectations are, and they must beware of their own biases. Assessing people purely on the basis of how they look or what their background is leads to mistakes, and leaders need to question their own assumptions about the roles other people play. I once interviewed a leader in a large and very formal professional services organisation who described meeting a newly hired team manager who wore a purple suit and had shoulder-length hair. The leader's first reaction was to ask himself what on earth this weird person was doing in the organisation.

He spoke to the manager, who turned out to be highly intelligent with a PhD in astrophysics, and whose mastery of his subject had already won the trust of his team. The leader changed his mind about the manager at once (although he did persuade the manager to wear a more sober suit).

To sum up, then, roles are defined in part by our own needs and in part by our reactions to other people and their perceptions of us. Leaders and followers should both be seeking to fit with each other and build a relationship. Most of the time this is what happens; examples of deliberately toxic leadership are fortunately rare (although they do tend to be the examples that stand out in our own experience). Much more common are problems of misunderstanding and misperception, fuelled by cognitive bias. Leaders either misinterpret the signals they receive from the organisation, or they make judgements based on preconceptions without determining the truth, or both.

This process is also dynamic. As the organisation changes, people's needs for leadership will also change. They may become more confident and want more space for themselves, or they may be uncertain and need more support and help. We can never assume that what people expect today is what they will need tomorrow.

GENERAL SMITH

Major-General John Smith (not his real name) was a successful army commander who had won the respect of the officers and men who served under him. He was perceived as tough, but fair. His style was direct and occasionally outspoken: 'I say what I think' was one of his mottoes. His style had been successful: he had reorganised the army's training command to make it more efficient and raise standards of training, and in front-line deployments he had looked after his men and directed them to achieve their objectives with minimal casualties.

After retiring from the army, General Smith looked around for another job. A hospital trust in the National Health Service was looking for a new chair on its board and approached Smith and offered him the job. The trust had problems with efficiency and poor staff morale caused by staff shortages; the remaining staff were overworked and struggling. The executives and other board members knew Smith's reputation and thought that he would be the right man to turn things around.

Settling into his new job, Smith did not change his style and approach. He continued to be direct and outspoken. He thought he was being blunt and to the point, but staff thought he was being rude and was criticising them. He did not offer words of praise when things went right because he didn't think he had to: why would you praise people for doing the jobs they were paid to do? As for staff shortages, people would just have to work harder still to plug the gaps.

One of the senior consultants at the hospital eventually took Smith to one side. 'You need to change your approach,' the consultant said. 'You're not in the army now. Barking orders at people won't work here. People are stressed and on edge. You have to treat them gently and with kindness if you want to get the best out of them.'

Smith was horrified by the consultant's words. 'I am not an unkind person,' he protested. 'I want what is the best for our people, of course. But I can't help the way I speak and act. I am who I am.' Although Smith was genuinely upset by what the consultant said, he could not change his behaviour. Eventually he was forced to retire from the job. His insistence that he had to remain authentic harmed both the organisation and himself.

ROLE CONFLICT

The idea that we play many different roles raises the possibility of conflict between these roles. Sometimes, the demands of different roles may conflict with each other, and this can be both a difficult practical problem to solve and a challenge to our authenticity and our sense of who we are. The sociologist Robert K. Merton defined two different kinds of role conflict, *interpersonal conflict* and *intrapersonal conflict*.

Interpersonal conflict arises when our expectations of our role clash with others' expectations of what role we should be playing. The case of General Smith is illustrative of this. Smith thought that his followers in the NHS needed the same thing as his followers in the army: directness and plain speaking. His followers, who were exhausted and stressed, wanted a leader who would be supportive and caring. That role conflict played a central role in Smith's failure as a leader.

Most interpersonal role conflicts are the result of the kinds of misunderstandings we discussed above. Leaders can resolve role conflicts by going into the leadership space, meeting followers and discussing candidly what each needs from the other. Trust and a sense of psychological safety are important to ensure that honest opinions can be exchanged. Once the leader understands better what followers expect, they then have the option of adapting their role (see below).

Intrapersonal conflicts are more difficult to resolve and potentially more damaging for leaders themselves. Intrapersonal conflicts happen when leaders face conflicting demands from different roles which challenge their own values. An all-too-common example of intrapersonal conflict for more senior leaders is the conflict between their roles at work and in their families. There are time pressures here, of course – busy senior leaders often struggle to make time for their families – but the psychological pressures of role conflict go deeper than just time stress. A chief executive might spend ten or twelve hours a day shouldering responsibilities, making tough decisions, being decisive and firm, but when they finally get home they are expected to be loving and caring parents and partners. Some find it very difficult to transition between these roles; when they reach home, they cannot switch off. That creates friction with their families, and still more personal stress for the leaders themselves.

THE PARADOX OF ROLES AND EXPECTATIONS

Following on from the paradox of roles and authenticity, the expectations of others can challenge what authenticity really means. We have to play roles in such a way that we remain true to ourselves, but followers may expect things from us that make us uncomfortable or feel like we are not being true to our own values. We said earlier that followers respect authenticity, but their perceptions of what constitutes authentic behaviour may not be the same as our own.

THE *BOUNTY*

HMS *Bounty*, a Royal Navy vessel under the command of Lieutenant William Bligh, was sent to the South Pacific in 1787, partly to gather scientific data but with the primary objective of transplanting breadfruit seedlings from Tahiti to the West Indies (the aim was to grow breadfruit which would provide cheap food for slaves on the sugar plantations). The voyage from Britain to Tahiti took a year and involved considerable hardship.

Bligh was one of the best sailors and navigators in the navy, respected by his crew for his skills. He was a strict officer who believed in discipline, but he also cared for his crew. He was one of the first officers in the navy to prescribe the drinking of lemon or lime juice as a preventative to avoid scurvy. His crew didn't like the juice, but Bligh ordered them to drink it anyway. Despite their continued respect for Bligh as a sailor, many of the crew resented Bligh's authoritarian ways. Bligh's deputy, Acting Lieutenant Fletcher Christian, was a friend of Bligh and supported him, but he also tried to soften the impact of Bligh's manner and make things easier for the crew.

The *Bounty* spent several months in Tahiti and the crew were allowed to go on shore. After the long voyage, the warmth and sunlight, good food and friendly people were like paradise. The crew did not want to leave. When Bligh ordered them back on board, their resentment increased still further. Some began plotting against Bligh, and they invited Fletcher Christian to be their leader.

Several fundamental role conflicts were evident here. Bligh knew that the crew wanted to remain longer in Tahiti; their expectation of him was that they should be allowed a comfortable life. Bligh, however, was conscious of his own responsibilities as captain and the orders from his own leaders that had to be obeyed. There were also dissensions among the crew, some of whom regarded Bligh as their leader and were prepared to follow him, while others were prepared to remove him from authority because he would not give them what they wanted. Finally, Fletcher Christian had an intrapersonal role conflict between his role as a navy officer and friend of the captain, and his desire to be liked and respected by the crew. He finally chose to accept the crew's offer of leadership.

On 28 April 1789, Christian and the mutineers seized control of the ship and forced Bligh and the loyal sailors to sail away in small boats with very little food or water. The expectation was that they would soon die at sea. In fact, Bligh used his exceptional skills as a sailor and a leader to sail his boats around four thousand miles to safety, losing only one man along the way. Christian, by contrast, was unable to unite the mutineers, who fled for safety to Pitcairn Island in the eastern Pacific. He was reportedly killed during a dispute between his followers. Most of the other mutineers died as well.

Bligh's refusal to give in to the demands of the sailors led to the mutiny and ultimately to the deaths of Fletcher Christian and many others. Had he done what the sailors wanted, however, he would have disobeyed orders and put his own career and possibly his life in jeopardy. He refused to adapt. Christian, on the other hand, did change his role but it cost him his life.

Adapting a leader's role to meet the demands of followers is not simply a matter of doing whatever followers want, because sometimes what followers want is not the right thing. We come back to the paradox: leaders need to adapt, but they also need to be true to their own values, to know when and how far to adapt, and when to draw a line.

ROLES AND AUTHENTICITY

The conflict between the demands of the roles we play and the need to be true to ourselves is a conflict we all face. But this conflict is particularly acute for leaders because how well they understand and manage this conflict has an important impact on the success or failure of the organisations for which they are responsible.

Chamorro-Premuzic argued that leaders should forget about the authenticity and concentrate on being adaptable, but that is problematic on two levels. First, leaders who are endlessly adaptable risk losing sight of what they really believe in, as the example of Fletcher Christian shows. This risks them losing sight of their moral compass and the possibility of drift into unethical and illegal behaviour (as we will see in the next chapter). And second, as we have already said, followers want to know what their leaders stand for. Lieutenant Bligh gave the loyal members of his crew belief that they would reach safety, and with one exception they did. Fletcher Christian gave his followers no certainty, and they died.

Earlier we mentioned actors playing a part. Actors are familiar with this conflict, and good actors know how to live with the paradox. One of the leading actors of her generation, Dame Judi Dench, winner of an Academy Award and famous for her role as M in the James Bond franchise, was once questioned about this in an interview. Her response was that every role she played also contained something of herself. This explains why different actors will play the same role in different ways; every actor who plays Hamlet is speaking the same lines, but they are also expressing themselves.

Many other actors have said similar things, and being authentic is seen as crucial to good acting. Sometimes they make only minimal efforts to disguise who they are. Sir Sean Connery played secret agents, outlaws, kings and archaeologists through his long career, but rarely changed his appearance or his accent; he was identifiably Sean Connery and yet he was entirely believable in these roles. Actors do not bring their whole selves to each role; instead, in each case they portray some facet of themselves.

Leaders can learn from this: to play a role, you also have to be authentic and open up some aspect of your authentic self. Doing this requires a great deal of self-knowledge. Take again the example of the CEO who is experiencing role conflict between their roles as leader and member of a family. Leadership requires concentration and strength, while being part of a family requires empathy, compassion and kindness. But at some points the opposite is true. In times of crisis, such as the loss of a family member, being strong will help the rest of the family, but there are also times when followers will require empathy and compassion. The challenge is to know which facet to show, and when.

JACINDA ARDERN

Ardern, who was prime minister of New Zealand from 2017 to 2023, won respect around the world as an authentic leader. As we said above, there is no such thing as a truly authentic leader, but Ardern's example shows how authenticity can be reflected in different fashions in different roles.

In 2019, a terrorist attack on a mosque in Christchurch killed fifty-one people and left many more injured. Ardern was widely praised, including by her political opponents, for the compassion she demonstrated, particularly when visiting the mosque a few days later and embracing families of the victims with tears on her face. Her grief on behalf of the victims and families was very real and moving. At the same time she showed she could also be tough, as evidenced in a famous speech when she declared: 'Speak the names of those who were lost rather than the name of the man who took them. He will, when I speak, be nameless.'

In 2020, when the Covid-19 pandemic broke out, Ardern again demonstrated her toughness. While many other governments debated how to respond to the pandemic, Ardern took swift action, first instituting a quarantine for anyone entering the country and, a few days later, closing the borders entirely. Later studies suggested that her action may have saved as many as eighty thousand lives. But the compassion was there too: she used interviews and social media to send constant messages to the population, reassuring them but also sharing their fears, speaking candidly about her worries for her own family. Her efforts were later described as a masterclass in crisis communication.

Two sides of Ardern, compassion and toughness, came together in her role. Both were authentic parts of her personality, but she wove them into the roles she played with great effect.

ROLES IN ORGANISATIONS

Thus far in this chapter we have been discussing authenticity and role theory in fairly theoretical terms. How can leaders understand what roles to play in organisations, and just as importantly, when to move from one role to the other?

The answer is, as ever, that it depends on the situation. Part of the skill of leadership is reading the situation and knowing what role to adopt, while at the same time being authentic and true to oneself and one's own values.

To give an example of how to adapt, let us go back to the situation graphic in the previous chapter and look again at the four types of action: *preparation*, *observation*, *intervention* and *participation*.

Preparation (needed when there is low external pressure and also a low capacity for response).

Roles that can be played:

TRAINER: someone who provides knowledge and skills to others, freely and willingly.

COACH: someone who gives other people confidence and a belief that they can succeed.

MENTOR: someone who shows experience and wisdom and helps other people develop their own leadership skills.

INTERPRETER: someone who can clarify complex or confusing situations and help less experienced followers to understand them.

Authentic characteristics required: compassion, empathy and understanding, a desire to help others develop and grow.

Observation (needed when there is low external pressure and a high capacity for response).

Roles that can be played:

RESERVE: someone who is willing to wait and watch, not moving until they are called upon.

CRITICAL FRIEND: someone who can ask analytical questions and help followers make better decisions.

PROVIDER OF RESOURCES: a function, but also a role: the provider locates resources and shares them, freely and willingly.

HELPFUL MONITOR: a second pair of eyes and ears, whom followers can turn to in order to check or verify what they are doing.

'UMBRELLA': referred to earlier, a leader who shields the team and protects them, letting them get on with their jobs.

Authentic characteristics required: patience, clarity of vision, humility (knowing that other people may know more than you do), a readiness to let other people succeed.

Intervention (necessary when there is high external pressure but only a low capacity for response).

Roles that can be played:

TRAINER: someone who provides knowledge and skills to others, freely and willingly.
INTERPRETER: someone who can clarify complex or confusing situations and help less experienced followers to understand them.
COACH: someone who gives other people confidence and a belief that they can succeed.
SCOUT: someone who gathers data or information and brings it back to the team before moving to an interpreter role.

Authentic characteristics required: decisiveness, strength, courage, knowing the right thing to do, the ability to withstand pressure, knowing your own strengths, strong sense of purpose.

Participation (needed when there is high external pressure but also a high capacity for response).

WORKER: someone who sets their leadership position aside and joins in the work on an equal basis with everyone else.
COACH: someone who gives other people confidence and a belief that they can succeed.
PROVIDER OF RESOURCES: a function, but also a role: the provider locates resources and shares them, freely and willingly.
CRITICAL FRIEND: someone who can ask analytical questions and help followers make better decisions.

Authentic characteristics required: willingness to help others, humility (knowing that other people may know more than you do), clarity of vision, knowing your own strengths, strong sense of purpose.

Several points need to be made about the list above. First, it is far from exhaustive. Depending on the situation, other roles may be required. Second, though, it can be seen that some roles will be the same in different situations, although perhaps they will be framed or expressed differently.

For example, there is a lot of crossover between preparation and intervention: the latter may need more active involvement in terms of helping people to gather data and understand the situation, but the emphasis should still be on helping people to learn how to confront the situation and achieve goals for themselves, rather than jumping in and doing the task for them. In times of crisis the latter will be tempting, but that temptation should be avoided. Followers will learn nothing, and the leader is likely to become overstretched and too focused on a few tasks while other more important needs go unmet.

To carry out these roles, leaders will need to dip into the various facets of their authentic selves. It is unlikely that every leader will have all of these aspects to their selves; paragons who can be everything to everyone are very rare. What we can do, as we will see in the next chapter, is reflect on which aspects need more development and work on ways of strengthening them. Coaching and mentoring are important leadership roles, but leaders also need their own coaches and mentors and critical friends to guide and strengthen them.

COGNITIVE BIAS

The final point to be made in this chapter is about cognitive bias. This is not part of either authenticity or role theory, but bias can affect our perception of what is – and is not – authentic, what roles are expected of us and how people perceive us.

Cognitive bias is often defined as patterns of irrational thinking that cause us to deviate from rational judgement. That poses the question of what constitutes rationality, which is far too deep a philosophical question to get into here. Instead, let us consider cognitive biases as things that make us see the world as we want to see it, rather than as it actually is.

There are hundreds of identified cognitive biases, and we all suffer from some of them. Leaders have cognitive biases, and so do their followers. When their cognitive biases work against each other, misunderstandings are bound to happen. If leaders suffer from optimism bias, for example, but followers are suffering from pessimism bias, the confusion between them will lead to lack of clarity about intentions, confusion and even organisational paralysis.

- *Optimism bias.* We assume the best possible outcome, and that bad things won't happen. This is particularly common in high-risk situations. Unconsciously, we feel the need to reduce risk, so by convincing ourselves that the risk is less than it really is, we begin to feel happier and more comfortable. However, this leads to misperceptions of risk, leading us to do things we would have been better off avoiding.
- *Illusory superiority.* Referred to earlier (also known as the Dunning-Kruger effect) this is the belief that we are more competent and experienced than we really are. For leaders, the danger is that they will overestimate their own ability to understand and influence events and people around them.
- *The illusion of control.* Also referred to earlier, this is the tendency of leaders to believe that they can also control events and people around them. If they admit that they cannot control the situation, this can be damaging to self-esteem.
- *Normalcy bias.* We assume that things will stay the same and that nothing will change. Like optimism bias, this is an unconscious way of trying to explain away risk. If we convince ourselves that dangerous changes will not actually happen, we are happier and more comfortable, even though the real risk is still there.
- *Hofstadter's Law.* American scientist Douglas Hofstadter argued that things always take longer than we think they will. This too is a way of dealing with risk. The longer a task or project takes, the more risk is inherent and the greater the likelihood that something will go wrong. We believe we can accomplish tasks in an unrealistically short time because this seems to give us more certainty.
- *Inside view forecasting.* If we were behaving rationally, when making a choice we would gather all available information and make an informed choice. Instead, we tend to compare choices with other choices that are similar. If we own a car and are thinking about transportation, we will look at other types of car and make choices between them, but we will not evaluate other transport options like cycling, walking or public transport. In organisations this means we stick to established ways of doing things rather than comparing options.

- *Pessimism bias.* The opposite of optimism bias, pessimism bias happens when people feel that they are struggling. They lack the skills or resources of experience to get a job done, and as a result they begin to believe that they will fail. We see this with sports teams when they are falling behind on the score. Their heads go down, their shoulders slump and they believe they are beaten even though they might still have a mathematical chance of winning.

Cognitive biases are like paradoxes; they exist and we cannot eliminate them. We can, however, identify them and make allowances for them. This needs to be added to the long and growing list of things leaders need to think about.

The task again concerns both leaders and followers. Leaders need to be reflective and self-aware, and once again use help from critical friends and mentors, to identify their own cognitive biases, and then they also need to become critical friends to their teams to help them spot *their* biases. Both need to work together in an honest and reflective way to examine how they are interpreting data and making decisions. Are we seeing the situation realistically? Are we being too optimistic, or pessimistic? Do we have the capabilities to do what we want to do?

Cognitive biases cloud the leadership space and make it harder to understand what is going on there. The kinds of roles we play and the authentic self that we seek to find are both affected by cognitive biases and, at the same time, help to shape them.

There is an old saying in Buddhist philosophy: 'Don't always believe what you think.' Just because we think or perceive that a thing is true does not mean that it really *is* true. For leaders, this highlights the necessity of constantly stopping to think and reflect. Again, are we seeing the situation realistically? Are our followers seeing it realistically? Or are we making false assumptions about ourselves, and them? Handbooks and guides to reflective practice can be useful but will only take us so far. Ultimately, leaders need to stop and think about themselves and the kind of people they want to be, and that takes us into the next chapter.

FURTHER READING

Biddle, B.J., *Role Theory: Expectations, Identities, and Behaviors*, Academic Press, 2013.

Chamorro-Premuzic, T., *Don't Be Yourself: Why Authenticity is Overrated (And What to Do Instead)*, Harvard Business Review Press, 2025.

Ibarra, H., *Act Like a Leader, Think Like a Leader*, Harvard Business Review Press, 2015.

Joseph, S., *Authentic: How to Be Yourself and Why it Matters*, Piatkus, 2019.

7

ETHICAL AND VALUES-BASED LEADERSHIP

The title of this chapter refers to two different but closely related points. Values-based leadership can be defined as leadership that is based on the set of values that the leader and the organisation both hold, the things that are important to them. We need to remember, though, that values are not always positive: dictators and crime lords might well have strong senses of values. Ethical leadership is slightly different in that it focuses more on the discharge of moral responsibility through leadership, or in other words, leading in ways that benefit other people. (The words *ethical* and *moral* have slightly different meanings, but for our purposes they can be taken to be the same thing.)

Self-reflection and understanding our own values inevitably brings us to the subject of ethics. There are, as we will see shortly, differing schools of thought about what ethics actually is, but most approaches to ethical thinking argue that there are two dimensions: being honest and fair in our dealings with others, and being true to ourselves. These two dimensions are inseparable. It is very hard to be fair and honest to others if we are deceiving ourselves, and if we are dishonest towards other people and are treating them badly, we are not being true to ourselves. (There are exceptions to this, people who treat others badly because that *is* who they really are, but we will come to these in Chapter 8.)

Leaders have power over other people and are responsible for them, at least while they are within the organisation. They have

DOI: 10.4324/9781003496243-7

a moral duty, and usually a legal one as well (we will come to the difference between these two duties further on in this chapter) to provide spaces that are safe and will keep people from harm. This is not just true in the workplace: sporting clubs and organisations are having to come to terms with this too, even in contact sports. The rising numbers of legal cases against rugby and football clubs for failing to protect players from concussion damage are an example of this. This extends to mental health as well, and legal and moral responsibilities are increasingly defined as including both physical and mental well-being. Put simply, leaders need to take care of their people.

Beyond this basic duty of care, though, some approaches to ethics also equate moral good with human happiness. It can be argued that as leaders we have a moral duty to promote happiness among our followers through things like helping them to learn and develop themselves, and to find positive meaning and value in their work. We can recall Jamsetji Tata's view that what comes from the people should go back to the people many times over, i.e. the benefit and value that people derive from their work should be greater than what they put in.

What about outside the organisation? As a leader, I have no control over my followers when they step beyond the organisation's boundaries. If, when they leave work, they drink too much or drive cars too fast or gamble, do I have any responsibility for them? Potentially, yes: if their work is placing them under high loads of stress and they turn to alcohol or prescription drugs for relief from stress, then I and the organisation are part of the cause. The responsibility for well-being extends beyond the workplace. Not only are we doing harm to people, which is morally unacceptable, but if people are suffering with mental and physical health issues, this will affect their work and this in turn will have a negative effect on the rest of the organisation. If people are off sick with stress, for example, others will have to fill in for them, which will create stress for others and hold back work.

But what if followers are misbehaving for reasons that have nothing to do with the organisation? What if they are posting offensive or illegal content on social media, for example? If their actions have the potential to harm the organisation and its reputation, then as leader I still have responsibility.

WHO IS RESPONSIBLE?

Many years ago when social media was a relatively new concept, a professional services organisation learned that one of its partners was posting material about a client on his social media feed. That material was in danger of breaching client confidentiality. The firm dismissed the partner on the grounds that their actions were damaging to the firm and its reputation; if other clients learned of this, they might not want to do business with the firm. The case went to court, where the former partner argued that because they had posted on their private social media page and in their own time, out of working hours, this did not constitute reason for dismissal. They also argued that the firm was curbing their right to free speech, and that they should be able to say whatever they wanted when they were not at work. The courts disagreed, confirming that firm's view that their responsibility to their client was important than the client's right to free speech, and upheld the dismissal.

This example highlights two points. Ethics is not just about behaviour and actions inside the organisation; it has implications outside of the organisation too. And secondly, ethics and reputation are very closely tied together. Unethical behaviour can destroy reputations very quickly. (The professional services firm above had been lax about drafting contracts for its partners; in most companies, *any* disclosure of confidential information, anywhere or at any time, is grounds for immediate dismissal.)

This sounds like it ought to be fairly simple – do the right thing and encourage others to do the right thing – but a lot of questions immediately come to mind. Here are a few of them:

- *Who decides what is ethical?* Who determines what is right and what is wrong, or what is good or bad in terms of outcomes? Throughout most of human history, those decisions have been made by a small number of high-status heterosexual males, who determined what these concepts meant to *them* and expected the rest of society to agree. This itself could be argued to be unethical.

- *Do we have the right to impose our own values on others?* This is of course what empires have always done. The Roman Empire imposed its values on subject peoples with the aim of turning them all into Roman citizens. The British Raj in India and multiple colonial powers in Africa set about trying to tear down existing social systems and replace them with the values of the coloniser. By imposing our values on our followers – and by extension, imposing them on customers, suppliers and so on – are we not in danger of acting like colonisers, no matter how good our intentions may be?
- *What about dissenters?* How do we deal with people who disagree with us about ethics and values? The age of transatlantic slavery saw millions of people trafficked from their homes to plantations in the Americas. The trade was enshrined by law and supported by the wealthy elites, but there was widespread public opposition to slavery for hundreds of years and repeated attempts in parliament to pass laws abolishing slavery were in many cases defeated only by narrow margins. Should the dissenters bow to the beliefs of the majority, even when they believe the majority to be morally wrong? As leaders, do we have a responsibility to protect the dissenters and make sure they have a voice?
- *How far do ethical responsibilities extend?* Are we morally responsible for just the people we can see and hear, those within our span of control? Or if not, how far does the responsibility extend? To our own community? To the country? Are we morally responsible to the entire world?
- *And what about free will?* The principles of ethics will necessarily restrict our actions and prohibit certain behaviours. Is this consistent with our rights as free people?

THE PARADOX OF ETHICS AND FREE WILL

If we have free will we can do whatever we want to do, but ethics means obeying rules, including rules that have been defined by others. In other words, being ethical means we are no longer completely free, and therefore free will no longer exists. The philosopher

Immanuel Kant argued that because we have free will we can freely accept the limits placed on us by ethics, but this sounds a bit like special pleading. If we accept the restrictions on behaviour imposed on us by others, and by ourselves, then we have to accept that pure free will does not exist, and our freedom of action will always be constrained. Is this a good thing or a bad thing?

WHY WE HAVE ETHICS

The case of the professional services firm above helps to illustrate the point about why we have ethics and principles in the first place, but also brings into play the paradox of ethics and free will. Without getting too deeply into debate – this is a book about leadership, after all, not a book about ethics – this is a tension that leaders need to be aware of. Many organisations now monitor their members' social media pages to check that members are not posting offensive content or breaching confidentiality, and people have often been dismissed for doing both.

This brings us back to the cultural issue of individualism and collectivism that we saw in Chapter 5. Different cultures – national, organisational and sector – will have different ideas about where the boundary lies between personal rights to freedom and the needs of the collective organisation. However, virtually every culture has such a boundary: the debate is over where the boundary lies, not whether it exists.

We can observe this going right back to the roots of human civilisation. Examples of codes of morals and ethics include the Mosaic Ten Commandments, the Code of Hammurabi, promulgated in Babylon in the eighteenth century BC, and the doctrine of Legalism developed by the scholar Han Fei and others in the third century BC. In these three cases, the doctrines were also given the force of law, with established punishments for failure, but they are in essence moral codes. The reason why these and other codes were enacted is clear: they were attempts to bring order and stability and society.

What if there were no ethics, and each of was free to do as they pleased? That is exactly what the philosopher Friedrich Nietzsche thought should be the case. He criticised principles of ethics as artificial devices established by societies to protect themselves. Nietzsche was right to the extent that principles of ethics are implemented by societies, but the ethics don't just protect the society; they protect individual members too. For example, the codes of conduct that most businesses have in force are not just there to protect the business: they also exist to protect the employees of that business from bullying, abuse and harm, including by their own leaders. (How well the code is implemented is a separate, though important, point.) Without the protection, workers would be defenceless against their powerful leaders.

Another point needs to made concerning codes of ethics. Although the three mentioned above were given legal force in their respective societies, ethics and the law are not the same thing. A common error made by leaders is to confuse ethical behaviour with legal compliance: I haven't broken the law, so I have done nothing wrong. But laws themselves can be unethical: think of the laws protecting the slave trade, for example, or the laws passed in the USA and Canada during the Second World War, confiscating the property of people of Japanese descent even though they were American and Canadian citizens. And going beyond this, the law does not cover every aspect of ethical behaviour. There no laws protecting concepts such as courage, for example, or kindness, or honour, all three of which are bedrock elements of most approaches to ethics.

Ethics helps to keep people safe, but more than that, ethical behaviour also helps to build relationships and trust. This is why ethics is so crucial to leadership. As we have discussed throughout this book, the relationships between leaders and followers – the leadership space – are vital if organisations are to succeed and reach their goals, and those relationships are built on trust. We also noted that it is not enough to just talk about trust: leaders also need to behave in ways that will encourage followers to trust them. Ethical behaviour by leaders provides two benefits to followers: safety, and success, both things that followers desire.

When we speak of influencing, then, one of the things that will influence followers most strongly is ethical behaviour by leaders.

How followers define ethical behaviour will of course vary widely, but research suggests that they are looking for three related things:

- *Consistency.* Every case where ethical principles are concerned should be handled in the same way, and the process should also be transparent so everyone can see why decisions are reached. For example, if two team sports players are found guilty of disciplinary offences on the playing field, the referee should penalise both in the same way. To penalise one and let the other go unpunished would not be consistent, and this might result in a loss of trust in the system.
- *Fairness.* As well as consistency, the principles should also be applied fairly. No one should be considered to be above the rules or principles of ethics. It is axiomatic in most approaches to ethics that everyone should be treated fairly. Note that fairness is not necessarily the same as *equality*. In some cases, fair treatment might mean giving more to one person than the other: for example, the new recruit to a business might need more training and encouragement and a little more of a helping hand, rather than being thrown into the pool at the deep end and being told to swim.
- *Justice.* The outcome should result in a situation where justice has been seen to be done and the best possible outcome has been achieved. For example, when a company needs to cut back on its workforce in times of economic downturn the process of making people redundant should not leave the laid-off workers facing unnecessary hardship.

If ethics were a simple matter this would again be quite straightforward. However, there is more than one way to look at ethics, and each has its own implications for the three principles of consistency, fairness and justice. We will look at some of the various approaches to ethics now, along with the implications for leadership.

APPROACHES TO ETHICS

There are many different theories of ethics, but for reasons of brevity we will concentrate here on just a few: *deontology*, *consequentialism* or *utilitarianism*, *virtue ethics* and *pragmatism*.

DEONTOLOGY

Deontology can also be described as the ethics of duty. The word comes from the Greek root *deon*, meaning duty or, more literally, 'one must'. The most prominent exponent of deontology was the German Enlightenment scholar and writer Immanuel Kant, but versions of deontology can be found in Indian and Chinese thought too, going back in some cases for thousands of years.

Deontology focuses on right and wrong. It is based on what philosophers refer to as *moral absolutism*: some things are always right and some things are always wrong, no matter what the circumstances might be. Theft, for example, is never justified, not even if we are stealing food to prevent our families from starving. Nor does deontology make any differentiation on the grounds of agency. Who you are makes no difference; what is wrong is wrong, whether you are the CEO of a billion-pound company, or a worker on minimum wage.

Kant was also uninterested in the consequences of actions. He was suspicious of terms such as 'good' and 'bad', regarding them as relativistic. Nothing in the world, he declared, could be declared beyond doubt to be good. He regards the outcome of any morally right action as justified. All we need do is obey the natural law, and the correct outcome will be achieved.

PRINCIPLES OF DEONTOLOGY

- Rules-based
- Focus on right and wrong actions
- Consequences of actions are not important

How does this theory meet our three tests of consistency, fairness and justice? The absolutist view is certainly *consistent*, and this is one of deontology's strengths: rules are rules and there are no exceptions. But is it always *fair*? Kant gives an example of three people who are caring for their elderly mothers. One of the three does so because they fear that if they don't, people will criticise them for being uncaring and unfeeling. The second does so because they regard it as their duty: families should always look after each other. The third does so because they genuinely love their mother and get pleasure out of spending time with each other.

Of these three, Kant argues, only the second is acting morally. The other two are thinking of themselves and their benefit, rather than simply doing their duty. We can probably accept this where the first person is concerned, but this seems quite unfair to the third person who is motivated by love and compassion.

And is it always *just*? Another example of deontology in action comes from Han Fei, the ancient Chinese legal scholar. He recounts an incident when the Emperor of China was holding court in front of an audience of his people. A man carrying a knife rushed forward, intending to attack the emperor, but before he could do so one of the guards standing at the side of the audience chamber intercepted the assassin and killed him. The emperor summoned the guard and rewarded him for saving his life, and then ordered his immediate execution for leaving his post without permission. Han Fei clearly approved of the emperor's actions.

THE PARADOX OF CONSISTENCY AND JUSTICE

We know that people value consistency, and Robert Cialdini listed consistency of behaviour by a leader as a source of influence. But they also value justice and fairness, and these will sometimes conflict with consistency as the examples above show. We often think of the law as something that has to be applied consistently and with no exceptions, but most lawyers will say otherwise: applying the law in exactly the same way in every situation will result in injustice and unfairness. The leadership challenge is to know where the balance between consistency and justice lies.

The philosopher John Rawls attempted to moderate the more extreme aspects of deontology in his book *A Theory of Justice*. Two principles from Rawls's work are important for leadership. The first is the *difference principle*, which makes it clear that those who are at the most disadvantage – i.e. have fewer skills or less experience, are struggling with illness or family problems and so on – are entitled to special treatment. The second is the *equal opportunity principle*, which holds that people are entitled receive skills, training and other resources that will give them an opportunity to advance on merit. In effect, this imposes a duty of care on leadership: as leaders, we are responsible for ensuring that our followers are treated well and given the opportunities they desire.

CONSEQUENTIALISM

In contrast to deontology, the ethics of right and wrong, consequentialism is the ethics of good and bad. The consequences of our actions, not the actions themselves, are what matter. The morality of our actions is measured according to the amount of good that results, and how widely that good is spread. One of the first consequentialists was Confucius who, although insisting on the need for rules and structure in society, focused heavily on the outcomes that these rules would generate in terms of greater wealth and happiness.

In the eighteenth century the English economist Jeremy Bentham argued that the main drivers of human behaviour were pain and pleasure, and that the best interests of the people lay in maximising pleasure and reducing pain. Bentham recognised the impossibility of making everyone happy all the time; therefore, our goal should be to seek *the greatest good for the greatest number*, a principle that became known as *utilitarianism*, a kind of sub-set of consequentialism.

Pure consequentialism focuses solely on the outcome. The actions do not matter; what matters is the result. However, this too is problematic. If we take this doctrine to its logical extreme, then cheating, theft and murder can be justified so long as we can point to desirable outcome. Is it morally acceptable to steal money, providing we give it all away to charity? Is it morally acceptable to break the law so long as doing so will result in good for others?

Is it acceptable to break the speed limit in order to rush a badly injured person to hospital, thereby saving their life?

CONSEQUENTIALISM

- Consequences of actions are more important than the actions themselves
- Judgement of good versus bad
- Greatest good for the greatest number (utilitarianism)
- Ends justify the means

One of the problems with consequentialism and utilitarianism lies in how we define benefit. The greatest good for the greatest number sounds fine in principle, but how are 'the greatest number' determined, and by whom? Imagine that you are one of a group selected for a training programme that could lead to promotion: you are one of the greatest number. But when promotion comes, you are passed over: you are no longer one of the group. This happens quite often in large organisations, and can lead to loss of trust in leaders and in the organisation. How and on what criteria people are selected to join a group needs to be transparent.

As a result, consequentialism can often seem both unfair and unjust. If you are one of the group who benefits, you may well feel that you have been treated fairly and justly, but what about the people who are left out? If a company makes 10 per cent of its staff redundant, those 10 per cent are quite likely to feel aggrieved. Some of the 90 per cent who remain will be happy, but others may well feel sympathy for those who lost out. And unless the issue is handled with transparency, as above, some of the 90 per cent may well start to wonder if it will be their turn next.

Good and bad are highly subjective terms, even more so than right and wrong. The people who make these judgements often have an agenda, and others will want to know what that agenda is before deciding whether to heed their rules. If the agenda is the betterment of society or the organisation, we are more likely to comply, but if we perceive that a small group will benefit at the expense of others, we are more likely to rebel.

One of the challenges of leadership here is to ensure that transparency. The motives for actions need to be made clear to everyone, both winners and losers. Criteria for selection – who gets promoted and who does not, who gets made redundant and who does not – need to be set out, explained and discussed. All of this is necessary to build trust in the system.

ONEIDA

Oneida was an American company specialising in the manufacture of tableware (knives, forks, spoons and so on). Somewhat unusually, it had its origins in a utopian commune; making tableware was one of the ways the commune supported itself, but the business later became a separate company.

Pierrepont Noyes, the managing director, saw employee welfare not in terms of philanthropy but as a duty. He once remarked that employers should 'make no welfare moves from fear, but always and only because you believe that company success should add to the comfort and happiness of every member of the working group', and that 'when your employees really believe that you take a practical interest in their welfare and that you mean what you say, you will have acquired an asset money alone could never buy'.

Noyes also understood the principles of utilitarianism. However, instead of dictating to his people what actions would be taken, he involved them in decision making. During one economic downturn, Noyes called his workers together and explained that the business was losing money and was struggling. He offered them two options: to take a pay cut of 30 per cent across the board, with all jobs being preserved, or to make 20 per cent of the workforce redundant with the remainder on the same rate of pay as at present. The workers discussed the two options for some time, but in the end came to unanimous agreement to take the pay cut. The company survived the crisis and Noyes was later able to restore pay to its previous levels. By allowing his followers to be involved in the decision and, most importantly, to determine for themselves what was 'good', Noyes preserved trust and good relationships with his people.

VIRTUE ETHICS

The concept of virtue ethics is usually associated with the work of the ancient Greek philosopher Aristotle, especially in his *Nicomachean Ethics*, though very similar ideas can also be found in the teaching of Confucius, especially on the nature of virtue. Aristotle argued that behaving ethically is a matter of *deliberate choice*. All decisions have an ethical component, and therefore we must ensure that we make decisions in a rational way, considering all the factors and thinking the matter through before taking action. Acting on impulse means simply giving way to desire, and we are likely to fall prey to selfishness and other vices. Deliberate choice, on the other hand, requires wisdom and experience, what Aristotle calls *phronesis*, or practical wisdom.

However, even if we make decisions as a deliberate choice, how can we be sure that these decisions are ethical and responsible? The answer, says Aristotle, lies in the cultivation of virtue. He lists the virtues that a wise person should possess: courage, moderation, generosity, honour, gentleness, 'friendliness' (which we can define as sympathy for others, or empathy), truthfulness and a sense of shame.

Virtues guide and shape our mindset. If we possess these virtues, and refer to them when making decisions, then those decisions stand a far higher chance of being ethically correct because we will be starting out with a predisposition to act in a virtuous manner. In virtue ethics, behaviour and action can be deceptive: what is most important is the mindset of the person. If someone does not cheat or steal, does that make them honest? Not necessarily; they may simply not have had the opportunity, or not be willing to take the risk for fear of being caught. They may not have cheated or stolen before, but that is no guarantee that they will not do so in the future. A truly honest person, says Aristotle, is someone who will never think of cheating or stealing because they know it is inherently wrong. They do not make a choice about whether to steal or not to steal: the idea of stealing never crosses their mind in the first place.

VIRTUE ETHICS

- Deliberate choice
- Collect the facts, then decide
- Practical wisdom (*phronesis*)
- Cultivation of virtue

Let us look again at our three tests of consistency, fairness and justice. With consistency, we can see an immediate problem. Not all of us have all of those virtues, and there are clearly some people who appear to have none of them. Critics argue that this is the weakness of virtue ethics: people, it is argued, are inherently selfish, greedy and lazy, and when making decisions they will look out for themselves first and ignore everyone else.

However, if we set aside our cognitive biases about other people and look at the situation rationally, we can see that most people do not behave in this way (and if they did, as pointed out above, society would descend into chaos). There is good evidence that the virtues Aristotle talked about may in fact be hard-wired into our brains. In *Kindness in Leadership*, for example, Gay Haskins and her colleagues talk about the notion of our minds being naturally disposed towards kind acts and compassion. The economist Paul Zak has written extensively on the part played by oxytocin, a hormone that acts as a neurotransmitter in the brain. Put very briefly, if we are in situations where we are comfortable, the brain releases more oxytocin, which produces a feeling of pleasure and happiness. When we feel we can trust the people around us, our oxytocin levels increase and there is a corresponding increase in happiness; conversely, if we are suspicious or do not know who we can trust, oxytocin decreases and unhappiness sets in.

It would seem, therefore, that there might be more consistency than we think, and that Aristotelian virtues are present in most of us, at least in some form. But the presence or absence of virtue is critical to the other two tests, fairness and justice. If leaders lack virtue – if they are cowardly, greedy bullies who lack a sense of obligation to anyone but themselves – it is improbable that fairness and justice exist.

A great deal depends on the character of the leaders. We made the point in Chapter 2 that the first job of a leader is to grow other leaders. Virtue ethics reminds us that we must choose carefully when selecting those leaders, and look for evidence of Aristotelian virtues in those we decide to promote and trust.

PRAGMATISM

Deontology and consequentialism give us two conflicting views on what is ethical, the one arguing that ethics lies in the actions we take and the other claiming that morality is a matter of good outcomes. Pragmatism, which has its roots in the early twentieth-century thought of John Dewey and William James, argues that trying to separate the means from the end is itself morally flawed. Both the ends we seek *and* the means we use to achieve have ethical consequences.

Pragmatists argue that rather than adhering to fixed codes of right and wrong, good and bad, and trying to apply them to every situation we encounter, we need to make each ethical decision on its own merits. It is accepted that we can never know with certainty what the consequences of our actions will be, and therefore a certain amount of trust and faith are required.

We make the decisions we *believe* will have the best possible outcomes, knowing that the possibility exists that we are wrong. John Dewey argued that all ethical behaviour was in effect a kind of practical experiment. In every situation, we formulate a hypothesis about the right thing to do, test it, and then if it passes the test, put it into practice.

An important concept in pragmatic theory is the notion of *moral ecology*. Whereas deontology and consequentialism use a kind of 'one best way' approach, suggesting that there is only one desirable outcome, moral ecology suggests that many alternatives may be possible. The moral ecology view also argues that the presence of multiple alternatives offers us a better chance of coming to the right ethical decision. Only when decision making is constrained by lack of alternatives do we run the risk of falling into unethical behaviour.

PRAGMATISM

- Ends and means cannot be separated
- No hard and fast rules
- Each situation is different
- Experimental approach

In terms of our three tests of consistency, fairness and justice, pragmatism argue that focusing too much on consistency is dangerous. Consistency, it could be argued, is the enemy of fairness and justice, because if we stick rigidly to the rules we will end up doing things that are unfair and unjust to others. In order to be fair and just, we have to take each situation as we find it and establish what is 'fair' and what is 'just' on a case-by-case basis.

A pragmatic approach to ethics offers us choice; but can too much choice be dangerous? Pragmatism, like virtue ethics, seems to suggest that we know already what we should do, and it is down to us to find the best way of doing it, the way that will yield the outcome we most desire, out of a choice of many. That assumes, however, that we have sufficient judgement and wisdom to make ethical decisions, but wisdom, as Ajit Nayak pointed out in the *Journal of Business Ethics*, is often lacking.

This is in part because of the way leaders are trained and educated. We are taught to ignore the irrational, the emotional and the instinctive and concentrate on things that can be rationally analysed and measured. Nayak's view is that this makes leaders less able to make ethical decisions. Emotion, he declares, is central to wisdom, and it is through wisdom that we see the path before us clearly. A wise leader is one who is not afraid to go against norms and conventions. Being ethical is far more than just following rules. It requires us to step up and take personal responsibility for our decision and actions.

In summary, our four principles of ethics can be evaluated as follows:

Deontology	*Strengths*: consistent in terms of establishing what duty is *Weaknesses*: if applied without exceptions, can lead to unfairness and injustice
Consequentialism	*Strengths*: seeks to create fairness and justice through positive outcomes *Weaknesses*: potential lack of consistency, much room for interpretation in evaluating whether outcomes really are positive
Virtue ethics	*Strengths*: human virtues include fairness and justice for others *Weaknesses*: while most people do have some virtue, much depends on the character of the leader
Pragmatism	*Strengths*: fairness and justice to be decided case by case, with each case on its own merits *Weaknesses*: rejects consistency on a point of principle (but also a potential strength?)

BLACKLEY SHIPYARD

Blackley (not its real name) is a small town in the North East of England, which in 1931 had a population of approximately ten thousand people. Around eight hundred of these were employed in the local shipyard, which was the main industry. The rest of the town was dependent economically on the shipyard; the yard's employees spent money in the town's pubs and cafes and laundries and markets, enabling these other business to survive.

The shipyard had been founded in the late nineteenth century and had prospered through the First World War, building warships for the Royal Navy. The postwar recession hit the yard very hard, and in 1922 it was nearly forced to close. This caused panic in the town, for it was recognised that without the shipyard, the town itself was not economically viable. There was little in the way of social safety net in those days, and if the yard closed the population of the town would have to disperse to find work elsewhere. A thriving little community would be broken up, and Blackley would become a ghost town.

Arthur Lawrence was a successful banker from London, then in his late twenties. He had fond memories of the area, where he had holidayed with his parents and family for many years, and had a great affection for Blackley. A well-educated, honourable young man, he was also restless and looking for a change of career, something that would help him to do good in the world. He bought the shipyard, invested his own fortune in it, and build the yard up again, this time making merchant ships.

The Great Depression, which began in 1929, saw the world market for shipping disappear almost overnight. Orders for new ships were cancelled. For a time the yard survived by doing repair and refit work, but these jobs too began to dry up. At the end of 1931, Lawrence and his fellow directors calculated that they had enough money to pay the workforce until the end of February 1932. After that, the money would run out. With no bank willing to lend them funds, they would have no choice but to close the shipyard and lay off the entire workforce, with disastrous consequences for the town.

At this point Lawrence received a message from the Romanian government. The Ministry of Marine in Romania was asking for bids to build two small tankers to service the country's fast-growing oil industry. Building these tankers would keep the yard in work for another year, during which time the economy might improve and the demand for shipping would revive.

There was one problem: the Romanian government was known to be endemically corrupt, but Lawrence was willing to take the risk. He travelled to Bucharest, where he was welcomed by officials of the ministry. To his surprise, he discovered that he was the only bidder for the contract. But everything went smoothly. The Romanian negotiators were happy to accept whatever terms Lawrence proposed. At the end of the second day it was announced that the contracts would be signed at the Ministry of Marine at noon the following day.

At ten o'clock that night, two officials from the Ministry of Marine knocked at Lawrence's hotel room door. Their message was simple and blunt. Unless Lawrence provided a bribe of £20,000, half to the

Minister of Marine and half to themselves, before noon tomorrow, the contract would not be signed. There would be no deal. A telegraph line would be held open for Lawrence to contact his bank and arrange a wire transfer, but he would not be permitted to make a telephone call or contact his associates back in Blackley. He had only a few hours, on his own, to decide.

The choice was grim. He could pay the bribe, and hope the officials kept their word and the contract would be signed. If he did so, the shipyard would have work and the business and the town would survive. But he himself would have broken the law; then, as now, British law forbade the payment of bribes overseas. If he was caught, he would go to prison, and be banned from ever holding a company directorship again. His career would be wrecked. And he himself would have to live with the knowledge that he had broken the law. And finally, he would have been contributing to and reinforcing the culture of corruption in Romania, which was seeing a small number of officials enrich themselves while the mass of the population sank steadily into poverty.

Alternatively, Lawrence could refuse to the pay the bribe. The deal would collapse, and he would return to Blackley empty-handed and tell his directors and his workforce that it was all over. In two months, the workers would be unemployed and the community would disappear. He would in effect have sacrificed the shipyard and the town to save his honour.

What was the ethically correct thing to do in these circumstances? What *would* you do? Think about it, and decide what you would do.

THE PARADOX OF RIGHT AND GOOD

Most of the time, the right thing to do is also the thing that will give us the best outcomes. But as the Blackley shipyard case shows, this is not always the case; sometimes, doing the right thing brings bad outcomes. Sometimes, if a leader does their duty, other people will suffer negative consequences. But if they focus on the consequences, they and their followers may be punished for not doing their duty.

ETHICAL LEADERSHIP

Although ethics is often perceived as a matter of black and white, in reality it is many shades of grey. Determining the most ethical behaviour or course of action is not always easy, and even if we possess all of the Aristotelian virtues, uncertainties remain.

There is no recipe or pattern for ethical leadership; it is something that each leader has to figure out for themselves. The twentieth-century French philosopher Jean-Paul Sartre once pointed out that we cannot expect other people to make ethical decisions for us; only we can decide what is truly ethical. That rule of course applies to individual followers as well as leaders: it would be morally wrong for us to decide what is ethical for our followers without consulting them first. (The fact that in the real world this happens all the time does not make it morally acceptable.)

This means that in order to lead ethically, leaders need first of all to establish what their own moral principles are. Where are your red lines? What things would you not do? What behaviours would you not tolerate in others? Use all of the four ethical approaches discussed in the previous section to analyse the subject and come up with your own moral code. Review this regularly: time, new information and wisdom may change your thinking.

Second, invite your teams to do the same. You can organise formal, facilitated events, have informal discussions and conversations, or some mixture of the two. This too should be an ongoing process, partly because views may change and partly just to remind people of the ethical aspects of their work. This ties very closely to values, as we will see in the next section.

Understanding our own ethics and those of other people should be part of both our own self-reflection and the relationships we build with others. Although it might be useful to have discussions devoted specifically to ethics, the ultimate aim should be to build ethics into our thinking so that all our decisions and actions are considered in an ethical light. Aristotle advised that we should seek to reach a place where we know what the ethical thing to do is without having to stop and analyse it. That will not always be possible, but it is a good aspiration nonetheless.

In practical terms, leaders need to ensure that there is an ethical component to decision making. The following decision-making framework – a simplified version of other similar frameworks developed over the years – attempts to build ethics into our thinking. Although there are a lot of questions here, using the framework should not take up a great deal of time; with practice, teams should be able to use this framework to reach decisions in a few minutes.

ETHICAL DECISION-MAKING FRAMEWORK

The framework consists of eleven questions. A brief explanation of each questions follows.

1. What do we know about this situation, and what don't we know?
2. What are our own loyalties and biases? What might influence our decision one way or the other?
3. What stakeholder groups are involved, and how?
4. What options are open to us? If they are unsatisfactory, can other options be created?
5. What issues of right and wrong are involved?
6. What are the good and bad consequences of these options?
7. Which option would yield the result that is most fair and equitable?
8. What do you want to do?
9. In your heart, what do you feel you *should* do?
10. Can you live with the consequences of your actions?
11. What will you do if it turns out your decision is wrong?

- *What do we know about this situation, and what don't we know?* Sum up the key facts in a few sentences. Why is this issue important? What matters about it? What problems do we face? What are the 'known unknowns'? Where do we lack information? There may be time to do more research, but if not, be aware that this information void poses a risk as we go forward.

- *What are our own loyalties and biases? What might influence our decision one way or the other?* Think about the cognitive biases that may be within the group. Are these distorting our perspective of the situation? Think too about the situation you are in and what impact that may be having. Physical location can be important. Research has found that if we work in a gloomy, depressing workplace we are more likely to be gloomy and depressed ourselves, and this can lead to a temptation to take the easy way out. A bright, friendly workplace produces greater confidence, and we are more likely to summon up the courage to do the right thing. Other research suggests that people are more likely to make ethical decisions early in the day, and that propensity to cut corners and take unethical decisions increases as the day goes on.
- *What stakeholder groups are involved, and how?* Think beyond the organisation itself. For a business, other stakeholders could include investors, suppliers, employees, customers and the wider community. How might they be impacted by what we are proposing to do? What might the environmental impact be?
- *What options are open to us? If they are unsatisfactory, can other options be created?* This can be trickier, because the pressures noted above can be inclining us towards a particular option already. Think about the moral ecology and try to avoid binary yes-no choices if at all possible. Try to generate at least three viable options and choose the one that fits best with your team's moral principles.
- *What issues of right and wrong are involved?* There may be legal issues, but once again, the law and morality are not always the same thing. What do right and wrong mean in this context? What does basic morality tell us we should do?
- *What are the good and bad consequences of these options?* We can run through these with each involved stakeholder group, and again, if we know our stakeholders well, we should be able to understand the impacts for them. What benefits will each group receive, and what harm might they suffer?
- *Which option would yield the result that is most fair and equitable?* Of course we have to ask ourselves, fair to whom? There is always a temptation to slip into utilitarianism here, but we need to remember Rawls's criteria:

1. every person has a right to liberty, but their freedom should never be allowed to impinge on the liberty of others
2. the least advantaged members of society should be protected as far as possible from social and economic inequalities

Rather than going for majority rule, think what result might be palatable to everyone.

- *What do you want to do?* Having answered the questions above, which option makes the most sense? Which do you feel is the best choice? And then, having answered this, look inside yourself and ask, *in your heart, what do you feel you should do?* What is your instinct telling you to do?
- *Can you live with the consequences of your actions?* This is sometimes known as the 'sunlight test'. How would you feel if your actions were to be made public? Would you feel comfortable explaining your views to your own family? Would you feel comfortable explaining them on national television?
- *What will you do if it turns out your decision is wrong?* In part this is simple risk management, but there are deeper issues too. If we make a decision that we think is the right thing to do in the circumstances, and then as a result of that decision someone is injured or killed, we have to live with that outcome. But we also have to recognise that mistakes will happen. We are only human, and as leaders we almost never have enough time and information to make fully informed and rational decisions. Risk is always present.

LEADERSHIP AND VALUE CREATION

Values can be described as practical statements of ethical intent. They are ethics translated into personal principles, which in turn inform our purpose and actions and behaviours. For Jamsetji Tata, his values focused on bringing prosperity to his country and making a positive difference to people's lives. Behind these lay a range of ethical principles including compassion and generosity but also a sense of duty; he felt, strongly, that establishing businesses that contributed to national prosperity and improved people's lives was a duty that he had to fulfil.

As with ethical principles, leaders need to be aware of their own values and try to establish common ground with followers. Recruitment of new followers should be aiming to bring more people with similar values into the organisation (although not too similar; if everyone thinks the same, we run the risk of groupthink). Sharing values can be part of the same process as establishing ethical principles, as ethics and values are closely related.

Having established what their own values and the values of the organisation are, leaders then need to think about how to put those values into practice. How they do so of course depends on the nature of the organisation. The values of a military organisation could be implemented through training and readiness to defend the people; the values of a police force could drive greater diligence in preventing crime and keeping people safe. The values of a sports team could focus on winning competitions, but might also include entertaining fans and keeping them happy, encouraging physical and mental health through exercise, supporting local communities, bringing more disadvantaged people into sport and so on.

For a business, putting the values into practice involves creating value for other people. At the Tata Group in India, we can see a framework which we have called *from values to value*. It looks like this:

FROM VALUES TO VALUE

Trust and service to the community

Building on the platform of values established by Jamsetji Tata, the group continues to be highly supportive of communities across India. Millions of dollars are spent every year on community support initiatives including healthcare, education, support for entrepreneurs, prevention of violence against women, the arts and culture, scientific research and many others.

To take just one example, the area around Jamshedpur in the state of Jharkhand has poor soil and it is hard for local farmers to make a living. Tata Steel at Jamshedpur provides healthcare and education services to several hundred villages in the area around the city. This is not seen as philanthropy, but is part of Tata Steel's business model; it is one of the reasons why the firm exists. As a result of this and many other similar initiatives, Tata has an excellent reputation in India and is widely trusted by the public.

Employer of choice

As a result, Tata is an employer of choice in India, and many of the brightest and best graduates of universities and business schools want to work for the group. Although salaries are often less than in other business groups, there is a 'halo effect' that goes with working for Tata. Because the group is perceived to have strong ethics and values, employees are perceived as having these ethics and values as well, and people trust them and respect them. This provides value to the employees themselves, who feel a strong sense of purpose and have high self-esteem.

Innovation and quality

Motivated employees are more likely to be creative and innovative, and to be focused on delivering quality for customers. Tata has several times been listed as one of the ten most innovative business groups in India. The company also encourages innovation and publicly recognises and rewards innovative people, even if they have not been entirely successful; it is recognised that we learn as much from failure as success. This provides more value and self-esteem for employees, but it also creates value for customers who received high-quality products and services.

Customer satisfaction

Because customers are happy, they come back for more. Research going back as far as the 1970s confirms that it costs much more to acquire a new customer than to serve an existing one, meaning that repeat business is where the real profits lie. This creates value for the Tata Group itself and its shareholders, which include several large charitable trusts.

Profitability and revenue

Profit can be returned to shareholders, invested in the business or spent on providing more community support. The main point to observe is that profit is the endpoint of the process, not the start. Profit comes out of the value that is created for communities, employees, customers and shareholders. In the words of one senior leader at the group, 'profit is a byproduct of what we do.'

This approach relies heavily on the ability of leaders to identify, explain, communicate and maintain the values of the organisation, and to ensure that their own values and those of the organisation are aligned with each other: that is, they have the same purpose and they believe the same things. Every organisation will of course do these things differently, but the two case studies that follow will give some examples.

Ethics and values are essential to building trust. Without trust, motivating followers and coordinating them to work effectively becomes much more difficult, even impossible. Followers are more likely to trust people whom they believe to have positive values and a strong moral compass. For leaders, the challenge is how to first of all clearly identify what their own ethics and values are, communicate these clearly to followers, and then find ways of aligning with the views of their followers so that all are in agreement about what is acceptable and what is not desirable. If this can be achieved, the organisation has a source of lasting strength and advantage.

H.J. HEINZ

Henry John Heinz started his first business selling food at the age of eight. He founded the H.J. Heinz company (today part of the Kraft Heinz conglomerate) in 1876. By 1900 it was one of the largest food-producing companies in the world.

Heinz's values were centred around the purity and cleanliness of food. He reasoned that good ingredients, properly processed, would keep without the addition of preservatives. His production lines were expensive and, for the day, high-tech with an emphasis on keeping out impurities and make sure food was safe and fit to eat. As a result Heinz's products were more expensive, but he reckoned – correctly – that people would pay a premium for the assurance of good quality. Heinz concentrated on providing value for his customers, but he treated his employees fairly and paid good wages, and was very conscious of his company's role as a citizen of the community. 'Humanise the business system of today', he once said, 'and you will have the remedy for the present discontent that characterizes the commercial world and fosters a spirit of enmity between capital and labour.'

Adulteration of food and drink by unscrupulous producers was common in the late nineteenth century. Salt could be mixed with sand, or tea leaves with sawdust, to bulk them out. Brandy and gin were often adulterated with cheap, dangerous methyl alcohol. Meat and fish were sold half-rotten. Outbreaks of food poisoning were common. A pressure group, the Pure Food Movement, was set up in the 1890s to lobby government for change. Most food producers opposed the movement, but Heinz gave it his public support. The other food producers were outraged, and accused Heinz of betraying them. Heinz responded that the standards the Pure Food Movement was seeking to bring in were what his company was already doing. (The movement won, and the Pure Food and Drug Act was passed by Congress in 1906).

Heinz's support for the Pure Food Movement and his company's commitment to good, healthy food, at a time when it was not always easily available, won him and his company many friends. Heinz was one of the most respected business leaders in America, and his company was widely regarded as a 'good' company. As a result, young people came to him seeking jobs, shareholders were always willing to invest in him, and his customers were loyal to his brand.

FAIRMONT YANGCHENG LAKE

Yangcheng Lake is a popular holiday resort near Shanghai. By 2013 there were more than twenty luxury hotels in the district, of which Fairmont Yangcheng Lake was the only foreign-owned hotel. Fairmont also owns or manages three other hotels in China.

Founded in 1907, Fairmont Hotels & Resorts has a long track record of working with local communities to achieve sustainable growth, and had been doing so long before 'corporate social responsibility' became a fashionable term. Part of Fairmont's global philosophy is the education of both staff and guests about the environment, history and culture of the areas in which it operates. This philosophy has been transferred to China and adapted to local needs. There are now major projects across all the company's properties aimed at conserving energy and reducing energy usage, reducing consumption of gas and water, reducing packaging, recycling kitchen waste and, where possible, using organic or sustainably sourced food in its restaurants. 'Green committees' in every hotel give employees a chance to develop and implement their own ideas, and also serve as a channel for staff education on sustainability.

Local sourcing is a key part of Fairmont's philosophy. Fairmont recognises the importance of its business to local communities, especially in terms of local purchasing, and strives wherever possible to purchase local products and to help the economies of these communities. Fairmont also collaborates with suppliers to help reduce their CO_2 emissions. Fairmont's Yangcheng Lake Hotel has gone so far as to develop its own vegetable supplier, Yangcheng Lake Farm, which is owned by the Kunshan city government and managed by Fairmont. The Farm grows everything from seasonal vegetables popular in Shanghai to Western herbs. More generally, Fairmont buys 80 per cent of its food locally, within a radius of approximately twenty miles from each hotel.

This policy provides tangible benefits for local farmers and supports the local economy, but it has been beneficial in other ways too. Food, especially fresh, nourishing food, plays a very important role in Chinese culture. The quality of fresh vegetables at the Fairmont has become a major draw, and the gardens themselves have become a tourist attraction. Guests now come out from Shanghai on special food holidays to sample dishes created by a specialist vegetarian chef. The hotel has also begun selling vegetables not wanted for the kitchens, running a vegetable box distribution scheme in Shanghai.

More recently Fairmont has begun another project aimed at restoring the old waterways and canals around Yangcheng Lake. In former times these waterways were a source of fresh fish, and communities of fishermen made their livelihood from fishing there. A combination of water pollution from nearby industries and general neglect means the waterways have either become fouled or disappeared altogether. Working with local villages, Fairmont is reviving these waterways and restocking them with fish. It is hoped that the waterways will supply the hotel with its entire requirements for fresh fish, and this too will assist the development of the local community.

Fairmont sees no difference between investing in communities and supplying first-class hotel services to paying guests. Both are part of its core business model. At Yangcheng Lake, Fairmont's commitment to the community is well known and admired. That commitment is one reason why the Fairmont hotel has prospered and its business has grown in the face of tough competition from numerous local hotel chains. Service to community equates to competitive advantage.

Source: Jia, F., Gosling, J. and Witzel, M., *Sustainable Champions: How International Companies Are Changing the Face of Business in China*, Greenleaf, 2015.

FURTHER READING

Aristotle, *The Nicomachean Ethics*, trans. A. Beresford, Penguin, 2020.

Haskins, G., Thomas, M. and Johri, L., *Kindness in Leadership*, Routledge, 2018.

Jia, F., Gosling, J. and Witzel, M., *Sustainable Champions: How International Companies Are Changing the Face of Business in China*, Greenleaf, 2015.

Jurkiewicz, C.L. and Giacolone, R.A. (eds), *Radical Thoughts on Ethical Leadership*, Information Age Publishing, 2017.

Kraemer, H.M.J., *From Values to Action: The Four Principles of Value-Based Leadership*, Wiley, 2025.

Lazari-Radek, K. de and Singer, P., *Utilitarianism: A Very Short Introduction*, Oxford University Press, 2017.

Leigh, A., *Ethical Leadership: Creating and Sustaining an Ethical Business Culture*, Kogan Page, 2015.

McQuade, A., *Ethical Leadership: Moral Decision-Making Under Pressure*, De Gruyter, 2022.

Mill, J.S. and Bentham, J., *Utilitarianism and Other Essays*, Penguin, 2000.

Nayak, A., 'Wisdom and the Tragic Question: Moral Learning and Emotional Perception in Organisations', *Journal of Business Ethics*, vol. 137, no. 1, 2016, pp. 1–13.

Rawls, J., *A Theory of Justice*, Harvard University Press, 1999.

Witzel, M., *Tata: The Evolution of a Corporate Brand*, Penguin India, 2009.

Witzel, M., *The Ethical Leader*, Bloomsbury, 2019.

Wu, G., *Between Deontology and Justice: Chinese and Western Perspectives*, trans. Li, Y., Zheng, Z. and Li, J., Routledge, 2019.

8

IDENTIFYING AND AVOIDING BAD LEADERSHIP

Most books on leadership concentrate on 'good' leadership, that is, leadership that helps to generate positive outcomes for other people, especially followers. Consistency, fairness and justice drive value creation and create happiness.

Thus far, this book has been no exception. However, we have to remember that not all leadership is positive all of the time. Many people – perhaps even most people – have at some time had experience of leadership that had a negative or damaging effect on followers and the organisation. Probably, if we stop and think about it, we will find that examples of good leadership outnumber the bad, but as behavioural psychologists remind us, we tend to remember bad things more clearly than good things, and so bad leadership looms larger in our minds. This can create another cognitive bias, where we associate past bad experience with present and future leaders: we once had a bad leader, so that makes us suspicious of other leaders going forward, and that in turn makes it harder to build trust.

Beyond this, there is the damage that bad leaders can do, often in a remarkably short space of time. We have mentioned that things like trust and culture are fragile, and can be easily broken. In large organisations where there are hundreds or thousands of leaders, a handful of bad ones can have a powerful effect. The incompetence or misbehaviour of a few leaders can become a form of contagion spreading distrust and demoralisation throughout

DOI: 10.4324/9781003496243-8

the organisation. The more senior those leaders are and the more authority they have, the greater the impact.

This chapter looks at two important issues:

- *Prevention*: how can we keep bad leadership out of our organisations?
- *Cure*: how can we get rid of bad leadership once it is inside the organisation?

The answer to the first question is simple (although not necessarily easy): don't recruit them in the first place. The answer to the second is more complex and difficult.

First, though, when we talk about bad leadership, what do we mean? We can classify bad leaders in three broad categories:

1. *Well-meaning incompetents*: leaders who have the best intentions but lack the skills, experience or aptitude to lead effectively.
2. *Sleepwalkers*: otherwise competent and effective leaders who lose sight of their own values and purpose, usually without realising they have done so.
3. *Toxic agents*: leaders who deliberately and intentionally do damage to their organisations and the people within them.

It should be said at the start that from the outside it can be very difficult to distinguish between the three, and there is indeed some overlap between the categories. Leaders who start out as well-meaning but incompetent can turn also toxic over the course of time as they struggle to deal with their own lack of ability.

WELL-MEANING INCOMPETENTS

This is probably the most common experience of bad leadership. Many of us will have, at some point in time, looked at our own leaders and thought, 'I could do your job better than you are doing it.' These leaders are not bad people; they are often very pleasant and decent human beings, and they may well have strong principles and values and a clear moral compass, but they have been put into a position where they are incapable of leading effectively. There are a variety of reasons why this may be so.

- *Lack of training or inappropriate training.* Leadership training can be a hit and miss affair. Some organisations are very good at providing training. Others are not, and this can result in the 'accidental leaders' we mentioned in Chapter 1, people who never expected to become leaders who suddenly have leadership responsibilities thrust upon them. Accidental leaders have to learn to sink or swim, and sometimes they sink. This does not mean that they are bad people or that their predicament is their fault. Their followers and the rest of the organisation have to deal with the consequences nonetheless.
- *Overpromotion.* Promotion is often based on past performance rather than future potential. The psychologist Laurence Peter observed that 'everyone is promoted to the level of their own incompetence', an idea that was later dubbed the Peter Principle. A leader who is struggling might have performed very well in their last role, but that does not mean they will perform well in this role, or the next role. An excellent team leader may be promoted to office manager and still be a success, but when they are promoted again to head a department or division, they lack the skills and experience, or aptitude, and begin to struggle with their responsibilities. They miss key things and make mistakes, and after a while their organisation begins to struggle too.
- *Illusory superiority.* Even worse than overpromotion, the leaders may *think* they are able to do the job, even when it is manifest to everyone around them that they are not. This is the Dunning-Kruger effect again: I must be able to lead at this level, or I would not have been given the job.
- *Fear.* On the other side of the coin, the leader may believe they are *not* capable of leading at their present level, and this fear hangs over everything that they do. *Impostor syndrome* is a form of anxiety that many leaders suffer from, leading them to doubt their own accomplishments and achievements and worry that their colleagues and followers will one day realise that they are not competent to do the job. Research suggests that most people with impostor syndrome are actually highly competent and well respected by others, who have no idea that their leaders are suffering in this way. Further, it also appears that a little bit of self-doubt is actually a good thing

because it leads us to question ourselves and keeps us humble. But too much self-doubt can turn into paralysing fear where leaders are afraid to make decisions or take responsibility.

- *Wrong fit.* The leader may have quite high levels of competency in certain fields, but not in the domain they are currently in. They lack the knowledge and experience they need, and their followers are aware of this and begin to doubt them. This is a form of overpromotion, but it can also affect sideways movement as well. If the head of an IT team is suddenly asked to take over a sales team, they are unlikely to do well; the cultures of the two teams will be very different.
- *Their followers refuse to cooperate.* Again, this is no reflection on the leader's competence in terms of technical skills, but the relationship with followers has broken down. Lieutenant Bligh, the commander of HMS *Bounty*, is a good example of this. Bligh was an excellent sailor, but he lost the trust of many of his crew because he would not conform to their expectations.
- *Personal problems.* Illness, stress, family problems and many other personal issues can affect a leader's confidence and erode the relationships they have with their followers. Often the followers are completely unaware of this and make judgements based on incomplete information. They may perceive the leader as being rude and angry, but this behaviour may be caused by some personal tragedy such as a child falling ill. The leader's behaviour does not reflect their true personality.

GENERAL SIR REDVERS BULLER

Buller was a British army officer who fought in the colonial wars of the nineteenth century. He was a very good junior officer, displaying competence and skill, and was repeatedly promoted. During the Anglo-Zulu War of 1879 he commanded a regiment of mounted infantry, again with great skill and considerable courage. For his actions in this conflict he was awarded the Victoria Cross, the highest British decoration for bravery. In a later conflict in Egypt he received a knighthood and was promoted frequently again, finally rising to the rank of general.

In 1899 he was sent to South Africa, this time as commander of British forces during the Second Boer War. Given his past record, it was assumed that Buller would defeat the Boers with ease. Instead he suffered a series of defeats and his army took terrible casualties. In his book *On the Psychology of Military Incompetence*, Colonel Norman Dixon describes how Buller became almost paralysed during one battle, sitting on a chair and eating sandwiches as he watched his men being annihilated. He was relieved of his command a few months later and given a smaller force to lead, where he recovered and displayed some of his old skills.

Norman Dixon describes Buller as a classic example of overpromotion. He was promoted in every case not because of perceived aptitude for his next role, but because he had performed well in his last role. A man who was very good at lower levels of leadership proved incapable of leading at the highest level.

PREVENTION

All of the problems listed above cause stress for both leaders and followers, and are things that should be avoided. Preventing problems from happening in the first place is usually easier and less costly than dealing with them once they have arisen. In each case, there are things that senior leaders should be doing to ensure that other leaders are not placed in impossible situations, and these things should be part of the leadership development process. Here are a few of them:

- *Appropriate training and support.* Leadership is vitally important and it requires investment and training. Promotion and selection should not be based on chance. Some organisations have well-designed leadership 'pipelines', identifying people with leadership potential and giving them appropriate training and experience that continues as they progress through the various layers. Teams within the organisation are dedicated solely to providing support for present and future leaders. This should be best practice in every organisation, no matter what size it is or what sector it is in. No leader should ever be put into a position for which they are not prepared.

- *Promotion based on potential.* We are often told that promotion should be based on merit, but the notion of 'merit' is usually based on past performance. People somehow 'deserve' to be promoted because they have done well. Of course followers who have performed well and made significant contributions should be recognised and thanked, but not necessarily by promotion to higher levels of leadership. Even if the followers themselves desire promotion, and have stepped up their game in hopes of securing a promotion, it is still not necessarily a good idea to promote them. Promotion should be based on potential, and this should be made absolutely clear to the entire organisation in order to manage expectations.
- *Mentorship and coaching.* These are very important for preventing both illusory superiority and fear. Mentors, coaches and critical friends can all help people to see themselves more clearly. If these services are provided as part of the leadership pipeline, leaders will develop a sense of realistic confidence, knowing clearly what they can do but also what the limits of their abilities are at this stage in their career. This will give them a firmer platform from which to build relationships with followers.
- *Ensuring the right fit.* The leadership pipeline also needs to include, as part of leadership development, an assessment of what kind of leadership people are capable of and where they will best fit. To continue the analogy of the IT team and the sales force, each needs a leader who can fit in with them and lead them effectively. Ensuring 'fit' is partly about what the leader needs, but it is equally important to consider the team's leadership needs at that moment in time. A young inexperienced team will need a leader who can coach them, an experienced knowledgeable team will need a hands-off leader who can support when needed, and so on.
- *Well-being checks.* In Chapter 7 we talked about the duty leaders have to their followers. Part of this duty consists of ensuring

that they are healthy and well and if not, finding resources or giving them time and space to deal with problems. This too should be part of the leadership development process: all leaders should be encouraged and empowered to check regularly on the mental and physical health of followers, and senior leaders should do this with the other leaders around them.

CURE

However, with the best will in the world, problems will still arise. Leaders will suffer from stress and burnout or be accidentally promoted into positions for which they are not suited. Training, coaching and mentoring can once again be deployed to help solve problems, but there are two other options that leaders need to consider.

- *Move people around.* Senior leaders need to watch the relationships between other leaders and their followers. If the relationship is breaking down and there seems no sign that it can be quickly repaired, the best option might be to move people to another part of the organisation. If a few followers are causing disruption to an otherwise harmonious team, consider transferring them out. Alternatively, consider the team's leadership needs and bring in a leader who can meet those needs. The people being moved may perceive this as being unfair or unjust, and they will need to be given appropriate reassurance. But the leader needs to take a consequentialist perspective here, and do what is best for the greatest number, which in this case usually means the team and not the individuals. Quite often, a disruptive relationship is a signal that neither party is happy, and moving them to another location will give them a chance to make a fresh start.
- *Exiting the organisation.* If nothing else works and the leader is still not improving or displaying symptoms of confidence, it may be that they are simply not suited to this organisation. They need to be encouraged to consider an exit. Support and counselling should be given, of course; in some cases, organisations will even help exiting leaders to find another job elsewhere.

When dealing with well-meaning incompetence, it is important not to attach blame for individuals. Quite often, the lack of competence is outside the control of those individuals. Care and compassion should be used when dealing with them.

SLEEPWALKERS

Stress and pressure sometimes seem like inherent parts of leadership. The demands of followers and their own leaders are often incompatible, the environment around them is constantly changing, competitors and rivals are threatening to undermine them and there never seem to be enough resources to go around. The chief executive of a company, for example, will be struggling with the demands of his fellow leaders who want more power and resources, workers who want more pay and better working conditions, shareholders who demand share growth and dividends, governments that insist on compliance with ever-changing laws and regulations, geopolitical and economic forces that impact on markets and supply chains, customers whose moods and preferences are always changing, and perhaps even other ambitious executives who are plotting against them in hopes of taking their job.

Stress distorts thinking and magnifies cognitive bias. We don't see reality clearly; we allow ourselves to think what we want to think, to minimise risk and hope that the best will happen because this will reduce our stress. We become confused, and we lose sight of our moral compass. In the course of doing so, like sleepwalkers blundering around a house at night, we cross over the lines of what is acceptable.

The work of William Harvey and his colleagues on professional misconduct, published in the *California Management Review*, shows how this can happen. When we think of executives breaking the law we often assume they are greedy, but Harvey et al. found that this was not the case. There *were* greedy people who were willing to break the law to get what they wanted, but they were a small minority. Ironically, some of those who commit professional misconduct are actually thinking of others and trying to protect their own organisation.

Recall the Blackley Shipyard case in Chapter 7. In the real-life version of this case, the owner paid the bribe, even though he knew doing so was illegal and he could go to prison if caught. (And he was: he was convicted, spent two years in a penitentiary and was disbarred from serving as a company director for life, effectively wrecking his career.) He was willing to take that risk because he felt a responsibility to his workers and their families; by, in effect, sacrificing himself he could preserve their jobs and their happiness. That does not mean that his behaviour is necessarily justifiable or that he did the 'right' thing, but it helps us to understand how extreme stress can drive people across ethical lines.

Harvey et al. identified four 'trigger factors' that help push people over those lines:

- *Fear of failure.* For some, the prospect of public failure is too much to bear. They worry that their reputations will suffer, that their colleagues and even their families will see them as failures and will turn against them; and sometimes, they are right to be worried because this does happen. Lack of confidence and perceived personal shortcomings and weaknesses also come into play; leaders who measure themselves against other more successful leaders can suffer a loss of self-esteem. Personal tragedies such as loss of a family member and the ensuing shock and grief may play a role. All of these things – and especially the combination of them – can lead to muddled thinking and a lack of logic.
- *Burden of custodianship.* As we saw in the Blackley Shipyard case, leaders feel responsible for their followers and their families. They grope for the best possible outcome, and either feel justified in breaking the rules or convince themselves they are just bending the rules a little and not really breaking them at all. There is fear here too, of course; what will the followers think of the leader who fails them? What would the shipyard workers have thought of the owner if he had refused to pay the bribe, come home and told them they were out of work? On the other hand, the workers might have understood and even applauded the owner for his honesty. The point is this:

the owner didn't stop to check what the workers wanted. He assumed the burden of custodianship with consulting anyone else, and took decisions on behalf of others because, under pressure, that is what he thought he had to do.

- *Inability to cope.* This is the extreme form of well-meaning incompetency. A leader who is perhaps a good person at heart cannot keep up with the pressures of leadership. Either they do not recognise threats and challenges, or they have no idea how to deal with them. Regulations and laws change and they fail to keep up. Perhaps they have little or no support from their colleagues and are left trying to cope with challenges on their own. Bewildered and not understanding their environment, they become unable to distinguish what is acceptable and what is not, and they blunder over the line into misconduct.
- *Ego and denial.* This could be seen as an extension of the Dunning-Kruger effect, a pathological over-confidence that gives leaders a sense of invincibility. They do not believe the rules apply to them; they can break the rules with impunity because they will never get caught. When challenged, they sometimes point to other leaders who broke the rules with impunity; if others can get away with it, why shouldn't they? These leaders were also heavily motivated by the drive to succeed at all costs; winning was all that mattered, never mind how. The ends justified the means.

Harvey et al. went on to point out that these individual triggers were not the only reason why leaders committed misconduct. Not everyone who fears failure or is overconfident breaks the rules; most people cope with their *internal* pressures and respect ethical lines. However, in organisations and environments where *external* pressures are also very strong, the combination of environment and individual triggers will push leaders across those ethical lines.

How leaders are incentivised and the targets they are set will influence leader behaviour. Sometimes targets are backed up by threats of punishment for failure. If a chief executive does not increase profits by a set amount, they will be fired; if a football team does not win enough games, the manager will be dismissed, and so on. This puts pressure on them to perform, and if sticking to the rules is not enough, they might break the rules in order to escape punishment.

Similarly, when leaders are incentivised to hit performance targets, they might be encouraged to break the rules for personal gain. If a sales team leader's bonus depends on signing up a certain number of customers, they will do whatever is needed to get that bonus. The payment protection insurance (PPI) scandal in the UK happened in part because bank staff were incentivised to sell PPI to customers. As a result they sold some policies knowing that the customers would never be able to claim, or signed people up to policies without informing them at all.

Another environmental factor is herd behaviour. In his book *Influence*, Robert Cialdini noted that people will follow the example of other people around them, especially leaders in positions of authority but also other people whom they know and respect. Cialdini wrote about this as a way of positively influencing people, but a much earlier author, the nineteenth-century journalist Charles White Mackay in his book *Extraordinary Popular Delusions and the Madness of Crowds*, gave examples of people imitating others around them, following them blindly into committing criminal acts and even murder.

The point to take away from this discussion is that people who commit misconduct or criminal acts are not necessarily 'bad' in an ethical sense. Pressures from the organisation and environment around the can drive them to commit unethical and illegal acts, sometimes against their wishes and their better judgement. Leaders need to understand these pressures and, if possible, take steps to mitigate them.

BARINGS BANK AND NICK LEESON

Barings Bank, founded in 1762, was the UK's oldest merchant bank. In 1989 the bank hired a young manager named Nick Leeson, who took up a post with the bank in Indonesia. He performed well, and in 1991 returned to the UK to investigate a case of reported fraud, which he handled skilfully. His reputation grew within the bank and in 1992, at the age of twenty-five, he was sent to Singapore to lead the bank's new offices there.

Once established in Singapore, Leeson made a number of unauthorised trades on the Singapore stock market that initially were successful, netting a large profit for the bank and a sizeable bonus for himself. Encouraged by Leeson's success, his bosses in London turned a blind eye to future unauthorised trades. Leeson continued to make highly risky trades on the market and encouraged his staff to do the same.

When these risky investments went wrong, Leeson hid his losses using a device known as 'error accounts' which held money to compensate for mistakes or delays in transferring funds during trades. This was a criminal offence, but Leeson was convinced he could win back the money he had lost without anyone finding out. He used a 'doubling strategy', a common (and usually unsuccessful) technique in gambling: each time he lost money, he would make another trade for double the amount in order to recover his losses.

In 1992 his losses and that of the office generally exceeded £2 million, increasing to £23 million in 1993 and £208 million in 1994. Leeson persuaded his bosses to give him more money, convincing them that his strategy would ultimately succeed. By February 1995 losses had reached over £820 million, more than double the amount of capital in the bank. Barings Bank collapsed and was dissolved, and Leeson was convicted of fraud and given a six-year prison sentence.

Elements of all four trigger factors can be seen here, but the strongest ones would seem to be fear of failure, and ego and denial. Leeson believed he could beat the market, but he was also desperate for his failure not to be exposed. Instead of admitting to his early losses and changing his investment strategy, Leeson concealed the truth for as long as he could. But the system of rewards in the bank, with large bonuses for high performance, was undoubtedly a driver too, along with the system common in financial services where traders have to hit performance targets if they want to keep their jobs In the end, the combination ruined Leeson's career and broke Barings Bank.

THE CHICAGO WHITE SOX

The Chicago White Sox were (and still are) a professional baseball team in the USA. In 1919 the club was owned by Charles Comiskey, himself a former professional player. A dispute erupted between Comiskey and his players, who demanded an increase in their salaries. Comiskey refused their demands. The players had very few options other than to agree, as the rules at the time did not allow a player to leave a team and join another without the consent of the owner, and Comiskey also refused to allow his players to leave. The team carried on playing, but the relationship between the players and owner had broken down.

One of the players, Chick Gandil, met with a professional gambler who offered the team eighty thousand dollars if they would contrive to lose the upcoming World Series championship against another team, the Cincinnati Reds. The White Sox were widely expected to win the series and the gambler and his syndicate intended to place bets on the other team at very good odds, and reap a large profit. Gandil met with some of the other players and offered them a share of the money if they would go along with the plot. Not all of the team were involved, and some only learned of the plot to fix matches much later, but enough were involved to alter the course of several games and the White Sox duly lost the series.

Rumours of corruption had begun to circulate even before the end of the series, and continued through the following season in 1920. Eventually the evidence surfaced and a number of players were arrested and sent before the courts. The jury found them not guilty, but eight players were banned for life, including one who had probably not been involved in the plot. The team became known as the 'Black Sox'.

With the possible exception of Gandil, who seems to have made the first approach to the gambler, none of the other players who were banned set out initially to commit a crime. Instead, like sleepwalkers they crossed the line without in some cases realising it. Bitterness and resentment against their leader was the driving factor. In some cases too we can see the herd instinct, players going along with the plot because their friends were involved.

PREVENTION

Preventing sleepwalker behaviour is first of all a matter of vigilance. Had Nick Leeson's bosses in London exercised proper scrutiny and governance over his activities in Singapore, Barings Bank might still exist today. Leaders need to be aware of what is going on around them.

However, this takes us back to the problem of the 'fog' that we discussed earlier. In a large organisation, such as a merchant bank, it is very difficult for the board of directors to be aware of every single transaction, or even the performance of every single trader. The distribution of power to other leaders throughout the organisation needs to also include a distribution of responsibility. Leaders at all levels need to be held accountable. Checks and audits can help leaders to understand what *has* happened in the organisation, but by this time it is often too late. It is more important to try to influence what *will* happen.

One way of doing this is for leaders to remind everyone else in the organisation what the values are, regularly and repeatedly. Constant reminders will help fix the values in people's heads and, provided they share those values, they will shape their own behaviours accordingly. When writing about virtue, Aristotle argued that we can become virtuous people by constantly practising virtues such as generosity, integrity and so on. Over time, these things become habits and we cannot contemplate behaving contrary to our values. By both communicating the values and practising those values themselves, leaders can demonstrate what is acceptable and remind people where the moral and legal boundaries are.

As part of this, leaders also need to care for the welfare of their followers. We saw above how trigger factors like fear of failure and inability to cope can drive people across those boundaries. No one, leader or follower, should ever be put into a position where they do not know how to do their job.

In his book *Out of the Crisis*, the writer on quality management W. Edwards Deming offers 'fourteen points' for leaders to consider. One of these, says Deming, is 'drive out fear'. Deming recognised that fear and stress can drive people to make mistakes, and he argued that people should be able to concentrate on their work without fear of failure or punishment. There is a counter-argument that *some* stress is necessary as a spur to creativity and innovation: if there is no stress at all, people can become complacent. Studies have shown that an element of stress in the workplace can lead productivity to rise, but only up to a certain point: after that point, productivity collapses dramatically as people are so stressed and afraid that they are unable to do their jobs.

Deming also called for the abolition of quantitative targets, believing that these too contributed to fear and stress. Again, some kind of performance measure is inevitable, as otherwise neither leaders nor followers will know whether they are succeeding. But when failing to hit performance targets puts followers in danger, the risk that they will commit misconduct or break the law begins to rise. Some American firms practise what is known as 'culling'. Each year, every employee's performance is measured against targets, and the 10 per cent who performed least well are fired. An employee who thinks they might be below the cut-off point may well be tempted to break the rules in order to boost performance and keep their job.

Prevention, then, should have two focal points: reminding followers of the agreed values so they can set their own moral compasses, and creating a business environment where fear and stress are less likely to push people to break the rules.

CURE

Curing the problem of sleepwalking is inevitably harder. If a leader finds themselves in an organisation where breaking rules, misconduct and criminal behaviour are taking place, the first step must be to determine whether the culture is *strong* or *weak*:

- In a *weak* culture, there is no leadership and no one is setting standards. People are aimless and lack guidance, and are largely unaware that their behaviour constitutes misconduct.
- In a *strong* culture, rule breaking is normalised and accepted. In effect, these activities are part of the culture and people are expected to break rules and commit misconduct. Those who fail to do so might even be punished by the others.

In weak cultures, leaders can sometimes change behaviours through influence and example. We saw earlier how in the Royal Air Force, behaviour at 242 Squadron was changed by the behaviours and actions of their new leader, Squadron Leader Bader. Dara Khosrowshahi, who took over as chief executive of ride-hailing service Uber after the previous leader, Travis Kalanick, had been forced to resign after a series of scandals, took decisive steps to change the culture of Uber. He made it clear what the company's new values would be, and that everyone was expected to abide by them, and over time the culture of Uber began to change. By contrast, at the American bank Wells Fargo, which had been affected by a scandal where employees were in effect opening fraudulent bank accounts in order to receive bonuses, successive leaders made little or no coherent attempt to change the culture and Wells Fargo continued to have a poor reputation for a number of years.

In strong cultures, it may be impossible to effect a cure. If a leader tries to bring in new and more ethical values but followers reject them, the only option may be to break up the organisation and disperse the people.

TOXIC AGENTS

In Chapter 6 we noted that authenticity isn't always a good thing. There is a dark side to authenticity: people can be bullies, misogynists, racists, criminals or even murderers and still be very authentic. Bullying and crime are their values, and by causing pain to others they are being true to themselves.

These people are fortunately quite rare, but the impact they can have on an organisation is severe. Toxic agents who create harm deliberately can influence the behaviours and actions of others, disrupt cultures, spread false information, cause harm to people and throw organisations off course. The more senior they are in the organisation, the more damage they can cause. Leaders need to prevent these people from embedding themselves in organisations at any cost. Unfortunately, this is not always easy.

David Boisselle and Jeanne McDonnell, who studied toxic leadership in the US military, identified a number of characteristics by which toxic agents can be identified. Among these are:

- They rarely take blame, and they rarely share glory. When things go well, they are quick to claim the credit for themselves. When things go badly, they will have a convenient scapegoat lined up, so that no blame attaches to them.
- They are not toxic all the time, or to everyone. When in the company of their own bosses, they can be charming and friendly. They can switch from one role to another very quickly, so that their bosses never see the darker side of their behaviour. Complaints against them from others tend to be dismissed because they don't fit with the boss's own experience.
- They are often intelligent and hard-working and have a reputation for getting things done. This too means that their own leaders will regard them favourably and dismiss any complaints. These are the people who get things done; and even if there is also some harm as well, it can be dismissed as a transaction cost.
- They have a clique of 'fans', allies who travel with them from job to job and act as facilitators. Sometimes these fans are the actual bullies or abusers, acting on instructions from the toxic agent at the centre.
- Someone, somewhere, has known that these people are toxic from the beginning, but they have been unwilling or afraid to speak up.

Other research by Gary McIntosh and Samuel Rima, and later by Adrian Furnham, has concentrated on the psychological underpinnings of toxic leadership. Seven archetypes have been identified, each of which explores the mindset of toxic leaders and shows the different forms toxicity can take.

- *The obsessive-compulsive leader.* Obsessive-compulsive leaders usually start off as micromanagers. They are unable or unwilling to delegate authority or share power, and insist on trying to control everything themselves. Anyone else who they suspect might also have control or power is either pushed to one side or driven out of the organisation. When the limitations of the span of control become apparent and the obsessive-compulsive leader realises that they *cannot* control everything, they become antagonistic, bullying and abusive. Other people are blamed for their failures, and trust within the organisation collapses.

- *The narcissistic leader.* Narcissistic leaders want everyone to focus on them. They are arrogant and egotistical, driven by the need for others to admire and praise them. They will never admit to making a mistake because this would be a blow to their ego. They surround themselves with people who profess to admire and praise them, and anyone who tries to tell them the truth is punished or driven out. They are not usually interested in building trust or relationships with other people, except when it serves their own interests.
- *The fearful leader.* We have discussed fear already in this book, but extreme fear can turn leaders into toxic agents. Fear of failure can drive them to take defensive measures such as criticising and attacking other people, in the hope that by pointing out the failures of others they can distract attention from their own lapses. Anyone who tries to push back or criticise the leader is, again, punished or driven out.
- *The malignant leader.* Some, a very few, people enjoy inflicting pain on others. Bullying, humiliating and abusing subordinates causes them pleasure. Often they become serial abusers, attacking many people across the organisation. Anyone who knows about their behaviour is threatened into silence or abused themselves. A single malignant leader can harm dozens, even hundreds of people.
- *The antisocial leader.* Similarly, psychopathic personalities may try to avoid having contact with other people and may react to the presence of others by bullying and abusive behaviour and even violence. It may seem strange that such people would rise to positions of leadership in the first place, but they are often able to conceal their real personalities when they have to. Once they have achieved a position of power, they let their true selves show.
- *The cynical leader.* Cynical leaders may once have had high ideals and aspirations, but over time these have been driven out of them, sometimes by other toxic leaders. They no longer have

values, and are suspicious of anyone who claims to be motivated by ethics or moral principles, believing that everyone else should be as cynical as themselves. They will break rules and take what they want without thought for others because they don't really care about other people or what happens to them. Their own gratification is all that matters.

- *The despotic leader.* Despots are hungry for power. No matter how much power they currently have, they always want more. They enjoy dominating others, but unlike malignant leaders they don't actually get pleasure from pain and suffering, although they are perfectly willing to inflict pain on anyone who tries to challenge them. This group in particular relies on cliques of other like-minded people to support them as they acquire more and more power. Anyone who refuses to submit to them is crushed.

The researchers are at pains to stress that these archetypes are not exclusive. Most toxic agents will exhibit features of two, three or more of these. Narcissistic leaders can also enjoy causing pain; obsessive-compulsives are quite likely to be antisocial, and so on.

Taken together, these attributes and archetypes give us a series of warning signals, signs we should be watching out for in our organisations. Preventing toxic agents from getting established in the first place should be the goal, but this is not always easy.

SIR BASIL ZAHAROFF

Basileios Zachariadis was born in Turkey in 1849 and educated in England, where he married and, in 1872, was arrested for fraud. No charges were brought and a judge ordered him to be freed. Zachariadis left England and went to Cyprus where he became involved in arms dealing and, allegedly, gun-running to Greek rebels in Turkish-occupied territories. He then went to America where he married for a second time and used his new wife's money to start a cattle ranch, which failed. The couple returned to Greece where they were confronted by Zachariadis's first wife, whom he had failed to divorce. According to some reports he bribed a judge to escape a charge of bigamy, and changed his name to Basil Zaharoff.

In the mid-1880s the Nordenfeldt company began selling the first modern submarines for military use. Zaharoff persuaded Nordenfeldt to make him their agent, and used his contacts to sell a submarine to the Greek navy. He then travelled to Turkey, Greece's enemy, and warned them of the threat posed by the Greek submarine, persuading the Turkish government to buy two submarines. His next stop was Russia, which had a history of conflict with Turkey, where he again explained the danger posed by Turkey's new weapons, and persuaded the Russians to buy four submarines. The commission on these sales made Zaharoff a rich man.

When Nordenfeldt was taken over by the machine-gun maker Maxim, Zaharoff persuaded his new managers to give him a contract to sell machines guns and other weapons all over Europe, receiving a commission of 1 per cent of sales. When Maxim was similarly taken over by another firm, Vickers, Zaharoff's contract was extended to heavily artillery and warships. Given free rein to use whatever methods he liked to generate profits, Zaharoff used the same system he had employed when selling submarines: sell weapons to one side, then go to the other side and stir up fear, causing the other side to buy even more weapons. He bought newspapers in both France and Germany and ran stories in each describing how many weapons the other side had bought. In one case he planted an entirely false story in his German newspaper describing a huge new arms purchase by the German army. The next day the French government voted for an equally large purchase for their own army. Zaharoff made huge commissions on all of these transactions and became one of the richest people in the world.

Zaharoff was not solely responsible for the arms race before the First World War, but he played a major role in it. The war itself led to tens of millions of casualties, but Zaharoff portrayed himself as a hero who had helped countries defend themselves. He was knighted by King George V and given medals by the French government. After the war, public revulsion at the number of casualties set in, and newspapers blamed Zaharoff for his role, calling him the 'merchant of death'. Undeterred, he moved to Monaco where he bought the casino at Monte Carlo and married a duchess. He died peacefully in his bed at the age of eighty-six.

How many of the archetypes of toxic agents can you see in Zaharoff?

PREVENTION

Prevention begins with recruitment. Some organisations practise what they call 'values-based recruitment', focusing less on recruiting people with the right skills and experience – skills, they argue, can be taught - and more on whether the recruits' values fit with those of the organisation. The recruitment system needs to be robust and use a variety of measures like interviews, psychographic profiling and interactive exercises to try and expose people whose values don't fit. The best way of preventing toxic agents from getting established in the organisation is to not let them enter in the first place.

CURE

Once established, the chameleon-like nature of toxic agents can make them hard to spot. As noted, they can change their behaviour. To the kings and emperors and generals, Basil Zaharoff was not a toxic agent, someone who was dragging Europe into war for his own profit; he was the person who could get them the arms they wanted, the man who could get things done. They had no idea that he was manipulating them by stirring up fear between countries.

However, toxic agents do leave traces. They may be fair-seeming to their own leaders, but their followers will see the other side of them. Here again, having good sources of information throughout the organisation in order to detect signs of toxicity is important. Put simply, leaders have to know what is going on their organisations, even if they can't be everywhere themselves. They need trusted and ethically motivated leaders and friends at key points who can pick up signs.

Once toxic agents have been identified, the urgent need is to get them out of the organisation before their influence spreads. A quick look at the archetypes above tells us that coaching and training will not help here. You cannot coach someone to not be a narcissist. Toxic agents need to be removed.

However, this is not always easy. As noted, toxic agents tend to be intelligent, and they know the risks they are running. Unlike sleepwalkers, who will stray over the line without realising, toxic agents know where they stand. They will either remain within the strict letter of their contracts, or they will conceal traces of their behaviour by various means including fraud and forgery, destruction of evidence and threatening anyone who knows the truth and might testify against them; including their own victims. Speaking personally, I have on two occasions been part of efforts to expose and root out toxic leaders. In one case we found evidence and were able to compel the person's resignation. In the other case, despite the fact that this leader's toxic behaviour was widely evident, they were careful not to violate the terms of their contract. We were unable to find enough evidence to dismiss them and ultimately I resigned from the organisation. One of the most difficult aspects of leadership is knowing that, for all our best efforts, justice and fairness do not always prevail.

SELF-EXAMINATION

We have discussed these three issues, incompetent leadership, sleepwalking over the line and toxic agents, as issues that leaders need to watch for in their organisations, and we have looked how we might prevent or cure these problems. But leaders also need to watch over themselves, and here again prevention is far better than cure. In fact, in some cases there may not be a cure. Once you have broken the law, there is no going back.

In terms of well-meaning incompetence, leaders need first of all to think carefully about their own suitability for any given role. This is particularly true of those 'accidental leaders', people who find themselves in positions of leadership without having expected to do so. Many accidental leaders actually turn out to be very good leaders, but others – too many – fail, often with damage to their organisations, their own mental health or both. Before accepting a position of leadership, any leader or prospective leader needs to engage in a process of self-reflection and self-examination, to see if they are prepared for the role. They need not be perfectly prepared; we learn a lot about leadership on the job, and good leaders continue to learn right to the end of their careers. But they need to be mentally strong and ready for the challenges they will face.

Any one of us could become sleepwalkers and find ourselves in a position where we have broken rules or transgressed moral boundaries without thinking about it. Self-reflection is again critical: are we comfortable with what we are doing? Will a proposed action enable us to pass the sunlight test? Surrounding ourselves with people who are not afraid to ask questions and challenge our behaviour is valuable as well. Critical friends will alert us to dangers we might not have seen ourselves.

We also need to be aware of how we are reacting to stress and, if necessary, take steps to reduce the stress we are under. This is important in guarding against both sleepwalking and toxic agency. Fear of failure, for example, can create stresses that distort thinking and push us into toxic behaviour. Burnout from pressure can lead to cynicism and a loss of moral values. We noted in the last chapter that leaders have a duty of care to protect their followers. That same duty of care applies to the leaders themselves. If, as leaders, we do not look after our own mental and physical health, we risk letting our followers down.

Sometimes, it can be best for both the leader and the organisation to walk away from a position of leadership and let someone else take over. We noted earlier that one of the first duties of a leader is to develop other leaders. This is one of the reasons why: so that in the event that stress and burnout become too much to bear, we can hand over to someone else and leave the organisation in a good place. No one will thank us for sacrificing ourselves.

FURTHER READING

Deming, W.E., *Out of the Crisis*, MIT Press, 2000.

Dixon, N.F., *On the Psychology of Military Incompetence*, Pimlico, 1994.

Furnham, A., *The Elephant in the Boardroom: The Causes of Leadership Derailment*, Palgrave Macmillan, 2010.

Harvey, W.S., Arora, N., Currie, G. and Spyridonidis, D., 'Why Individuals Commit Professional Misconduct and What Leaders Can Do to Prevent It', *California Management Review*, vol. 64, no. 3, 2024.

McIntosh, G.L. and Rima, S.D., *Overcoming the Dark Side of Leadership: How to Become an Effective Leader by Confronting Potential Failures*, Baker Books, 2007.

Peter, L.J. and Hull, R., *The Peter Principle: Why Things Always Go Wrong*, William Morrow, 1969.

9

LEADERSHIP IN PRACTICE

Ten Things to Do

Throughout this book we have avoided defining leadership, having concluded early on that a firm definition of leadership is probably impossible and may not even be desirable. Leadership is found in such a wide variety of organisations and across so many levels within and between organisations that a firm definition would probably not be helpful. Nor have we succumbed to the temptation to attempt to identify generic principles of leadership, things that characterise all leadership everywhere.

Throughout the book, however, we have identified certain things that leaders do, or should be doing in order to lead effectively. We can state, with a certain amount of confidence, that most leaders need to do these things most of the time. The context will vary widely but the basics remain the same.

The list below contains ten actions. The list is almost certainly not complete; as you reflect on it, you may well realise that there are other things you need to do as well. If that is the case, add them to your own list. The main thing is to make sure that you implement these activities and make them part of your own practice as a leader.

1. Reflect on your own values.
2. Reflect on your own ethical position.
3. Understand the leadership space.
4. Embrace paradox and think holistically.

DOI: 10.4324/9781003496243-9

5. Develop your own adaptive capacity.
6. Learn to trust and to build trust in others.
7. Encourage other leaders.
8. Think about how you communicate.
9. Engage in continuous learning.
10. Reflect constantly and encourage others to do the same.

REFLECT ON YOUR OWN VALUES

This is essential if you are to be an authentic leader. Every leader should know what they stand for, why they are a leader and what their purpose is. A clear understanding of your own values will provide the following benefits:

- It will give you a clear sense of direction and purpose when making decisions.
- It will help you identify what you do not *want* to do, where your true course lies and what dead ends should be avoided.
- If your values are clearly expressed and demonstrated, followers will find it easier to understand who you are and how to build relationships with you.

Failure to understand your own values can lead to the opposite of the above: a lack of clarity about what you should be doing, confusion about the best course of action, and a lack of understanding by followers about who you are and what you stand for. Followers want a degree of certainty about who their leaders are, and if you provide this you stand a better chance of building trust with them.

Values are the bedrock of everything else. Without strong, clear values, the other actions below will become harder or even impossible.

REFLECT ON YOUR OWN ETHICAL POSITION

From your values you can establish your own ethical position. Be clear about your red lines, what things you would be willing to do and why, but also what things you would *not* be willing to do and why. This becomes your moral compass, and in times when it is not clear what is the ethical thing to do, understanding your own ethical position will help you to chart a way through. Moreover, if you have the respect of the other people in the organisation, they will be more likely to follow your example.

- Behaving ethically makes it more likely that other people will trust you.
- Behaving ethically makes it more likely that you will make decisions that have positive outcomes for all concerned.
- Behaving ethically makes it more likely that your stress levels will be reduced and your personal satisfaction from the job will increase because you know you are doing positive things.

Again, a lack of understanding of your ethical position leads to the opposite: people are less likely to trust you if they think you are capable of unethical behaviour, you are more likely to make decisions and take actions that are fraught with risk, and your own mental health may also be at risk. We referred earlier to the role that ethics plays in holding societies together, and the same is true of organisations: if everyone in an organisation did exactly what they wanted with no thought for others, the organisation would quickly disintegrate. Leaders provide the moral example that others will follow for the good of the organisation.

UNDERSTAND THE LEADERSHIP SPACE

One of the first things leaders need to understand is that leadership is not about them. Followers are not there just to do what the leader tells them to do, or to make the leader look good. Followers and leaders are in a partnership: each needs the other in order to achieve their purpose.

This brings us to the notion of leadership as process and space, and that space includes both followers and leaders. Within that space, leaders and followers all need to know the roles that they are expected to play. As we saw in Chapter 3, one of the tasks of the leader is to make sure that this happens: that everyone is clear about the team's purpose and their own role. Within the leadership space, the leader acts as a coordinator who brings everyone together and gets the best out of them. Ideally the leader creates synergy, where the output of the team working together is greater than what team members would have been able to create on their own.

This requires a certain amount of sublimation of ego on the part of all concerned. Successes are not individual success, nor are failures the result of individual actions: success belongs to the team, and failures are the responsibility of the team. When failures happen, good leaders don't point fingers or assign blame: they conduct post-mortems and help the team understand what went wrong and how it can be repaired.

To repeat, think about leadership as process and space. Within that space too, you need to exercise that duty of care that we talked about earlier. Monitor your followers, check on their physical and mental health and make sure they have the skills and resources they need to carry out their tasks.

EMBRACE PARADOX AND THINK HOLISTICALLY

Leadership is full of paradoxes. We have identified more than twenty in this book, and that is probably just the tip of the iceberg. Remember that paradoxes are not puzzles or problems to be solved. They are logical contradictions that nevertheless exist, things we have to deal with even though they don't make sense. That is an important thing to recognise: not everything in leadership makes sense. Not everything is rational.

In order to deal with paradox, look at organisations as whole systems. If you try to lead by breaking organisations down into parts, you will come up against the paradoxes. Think about the whole system and see it as both rational and irrational at the same time: rational because it is logically designed, irrational because it is composed of human beings with cognitive biases who are capable of irrational thought and action.

Further to this, learn to see those systems as complex, adaptive and dynamic. Think of an organisation as a kaleidoscope where the patterns constantly shift and change. Individual elements of the kaleidoscopic pattern are just coloured blobs. It is the pattern that matters, but that pattern shifts and recreates itself on a dynamic basis.

As leaders, how do we deal with this? There are two ways of doing so. First, we rely on our teams; no successful leader leads alone. Second, we reflect and learn. We recognise that we ourselves are also changing, and we adapt to new circumstances. If we cannot do both of these things, we and our organisations will both suffer.

DEVELOP YOUR OWN ADAPTIVE CAPACITY

Many of us fear change because it brings uncertainty and risk. But change can also bring challenge and opportunity, and leaders need to see change in this light. One of the roles that leaders often play is as interpreters of change for followers. When change comes, or is threatened, followers look to their leaders for guidance. What will the change mean for them? Leaders can give followers the confidence to deal with change, but only if they themselves are confident.

Many cognitive biases – optimism bias and normalcy bias, to name just two – affect our ability to analyse change. Learn to recognise biases and adjust your thinking to reflect this.

The ability to change and switch roles is also part of adaptive capacity. Reflect on the roles that you play, and consider the paradox of roles and authenticity. How can you play different roles, adapting to what followers need from you, but always in a way that reflects your own authenticity and who you really are?

LEARN TO TRUST AND TO BUILD TRUST IN OTHERS

Within the leadership space, one of the critical tasks of the leader is to build trust, psychological safety and inclusion. We saw earlier how diversity is an important component of an effective organisation, but to make diversity work, leaders need to create a culture of inclusion so that diverse people feel comfortable working with each other. The leader needs to influence other so shape that environment.

Gaining the trust of followers, and persuading them to trust each other, requires time to create dialogue and build relationships.

Let your followers get to know you. Be authentic and lead by example. Use techniques like reciprocity, thanking them for their efforts and praising them in order to build up their self-esteem. Earlier we saw how Gay Haskins and her colleagues argued for the importance of kindness in leadership in order to build relationships and trust.

At the same time, as a leader you have to learn to trust others. The limitations of the span of control mean that you will have to distribute power to others. Because you cannot control their actions and behaviours, you have to trust that they will do the right things. Remind them constantly of the values and purpose of the organisation and engage in dialogue to ensure that they share those values. Ultimately, an organisation will not survive for long unless its members trust each other. Trust-building, then, is another key part of leadership.

ENCOURAGE OTHER LEADERS

One more time: one of the jobs of a leader is to develop other leaders. From the beginning, try to identify people in your environment who could also become leaders. Establish networks of leaders all around you, and then distribute power to them so they can get things done. No leader can do everything themselves, and attempting to do so quickly descends into micromanagement and obsessive-compulsion. Growing and developing those other leaders as early as possible is essential.

What marks other people out as having leadership potential? Quite possibly they are already acting as leaders in some way, helping and guiding others, supporting people who lack confidence and skills, and so on. If you can see that they are effective in these roles, try to develop relationships of trust with them. If this succeeds, you have a potential future leader. Keep working with them to give them confidence and experience and make them ready to take on more responsibility.

THINK ABOUT HOW YOU COMMUNICATE

When we think of communication we usually start with the content of messages, and that is of course important. Leaders needs to be self-aware communicators: that is, they need to understand how their messages will be received by followers and others. Will followers understand what is said? Is it possible that they will *misunderstand* the message and take it in a way that was not intended? Or will they look for subtexts, trying to deconstruct the message and look for hidden meanings or things you are *not* saying? All of these are possible and frequently happen.

Clarity of message is therefore highly important. How the message is communicated will also send signals to followers. A personal conversation, a formal letter or email and a post on the organisation's website will be interpreted differently and given different levels of importance, depending on the subject of the conversation. Generally speaking, personal and social issues are best handled face-to-face while technical changes to processes and so on can be put out on all-staff message boards and emails, but there are exceptions to both cases.

Communication needs to be authentic; it has to sound like you. Using jargon and corporate-speak will probably just confuse your audience. Speak or write naturally, but in a way that your audience can understand. And finally, communicate frequently and regularly so that your audience is reminded of the key messages.

ENGAGE IN CONTINUOUS LEARNING

The world, our organisations, our people and we ourselves are constantly changing. To keep up with change and understand its implications, as leaders we must engage in continuous learning. Formal training courses and programmes, webinars and seminars are one route to learning, but we can also learn informally by reading books and articles, listening to podcasts, watching documentaries and generally trying to understand the world around us a little better. We can learn from each other, too. Colleagues in the organisation will always know things we don't know, and encouraging information sharing is important. And finally, we can learn about ourselves through self-reflection.

Learning needs to be done critically. Check the authenticity of any source and whether the information it offers is verifiable. AI hallucinations are already responsible for a prodigious amount of misinformation on the internet. Use trusted sources and triangulate by looking at other trusted sources to see if the information and knowledge you have received are verifiable. Don't trust that any single source can tell you everything – not even this one.

REFLECT CONSTANTLY AND ENCOURAGE OTHERS TO DO THE SAME

Leaders are often busy and have many demands on their time, meaning it can be hard to find time to reflect and think about what they are facing. Nonetheless, this is a vitally important activity. Reflection allows us to:

- Make sense of new knowledge and information and put it into context.
- Think about the future and what might happen next.
- Think about events that have just happened and critically analyse your own and your team's response: what might you have done differently?
- Think about your own well-being and health: are you coping with the pressures, or do you need help?
- Think about your team's well-being and health: do you need to step in and support them?
- Analyse data in a critical way and think about what story it is telling you.
- Think about your own communication style and whether it is working.
- Think about the roles you play and how well you are playing them: are adaptations needed?
- Any of a myriad other things that may be important at the moment.

Reflection doesn't have to be a solitary activity. Bring your team together and ask them to reflect on these questions too. Gather feedback on your own performance, and offer feedback on theirs. Post-mortems, looking back at a recently completed project and taking lessons from it, are important sources of learning, but some organisations also use pre-mortems, analysing what *might* happen, creating various future scenarios and crafting responses to them. What happens if customers don't like this product? What will we do if a key player on the football team is injured partway through the match? How would we respond to the introduction of a new technology?

CONCLUSION

As noted, this is only a partial list and you will doubtless be able to think of other things to add to your own list. Doing this is strongly recommended, as you will be able to develop a list of reflections and actions that will be personal to you and your way of leading.

Ultimately, no one can tell you how to be a leader. That was never the intention of this book, and if at times it has come across that way, I can only apologise. The purpose here was to examine what happens in the leadership space and look at some of the things that go on there in a more analytical way: to explain not only what happens but why and how it happens. Hopefully by the end of this book you will have a better understanding of the leadership space and will be more confident about your ability to take your place there. If so: good luck, be strong and have courage. You will need all three.

FURTHER READING

Johns, C., *Becoming a Reflective Practitioner*, Wiley, 2025.

BIBLIOGRAPHY

Adair, J., *The Inspirational Leader: How to Motivate, Encourage and Achieve Success*, Kogan Page, 2005.

Aristotle, *The Nicomachean Ethics*, trans. A. Beresford, Penguin, 2020.

Belbin, R. M., *Management Teams: Why They Succeed or Fail*, Routledge, 2010.

Biddle, B.J., *Role Theory: Expectations, Identities, and Behaviors*, Academic Press, 2013.

Blake, R. and Mouton, J., *The Managerial Grid III: The Key to Leadership Excellence,* Gulf Publishing, 1985.

Bolden, R., Hawkins, B., Gosling, J. and Taylor, S., *Exploring Leadership: Individual, Organizational, and Societal Perspectives*, Oxford University Press, 2011.

Burns, J.M., *Leadership*, HarperCollins, 1978, reprinted 2010.

Chamorro-Premuzic, T., *Don't Be Yourself: Why Authenticity is Overrated (And What to Do Instead)*, Harvard Business Review Press, 2025.

Chilson, N., *Getting Out of Control: Emergent Leadership in a Complex World*, New Degree Press, 2021.

Cialdini, R.B., *Influence: The Psychology of Persuasion*, Harper Business, 2021.

Deming, W.E., *Out of the Crisis*, MIT Press, 2000.

Dixon, N.F., *On the Psychology of Military Incompetence*, Pimlico, 1994.

Edmondson, A., 'Psychological Safety and Learning Behavior in Work Teams', *Administrative Science Quarterly*, vol. 4, no. 2, 1999, pp. 350–383.

Ferrazzi, K., *Never Lead Alone: 10 Shifts From Leadership to Teamship*, Harper Business, 2024.

Fidanboy, M., *Organizations and Complex Adaptive Systems*, Routledge, 2024.

Furnham, A., *The Elephant in the Boardroom: The Causes of Leadership Derailment*, Palgrave Macmillan, 2010.

Goffee, R. and Jones, G., *Clever: Leading Your Smartest, Most Creative People*, Harvard Business Review Press, 2009.

Greenleaf, R.K., *Servant Leadership: A Journey into the Nature of Legitimate Power and Greatness*, Paulist Press, 2002.

Grint, K., *Leadership: A Very Short Introduction*, Oxford University Press, 2010.

Grove, A., *Only the Paranoid Survive: How to Exploit the Crisis Points that Challenge Every Company and Career*, Profile Books, 2022.

Handy, C., *Understanding Organizations*, Penguin, 1993.

Harvey, W.S., Arora, N., Currie, G. and Spyridonidis, D., 'Why Individuals Commit Professional Misconduct and What Leaders Can Do to Prevent It', *California Management Review*, vol. 64, no. 3, 2024.

Haskins, G., Thomas, M. and Johri, L., *Kindness in Leadership*, Routledge, 2018.

Hersey, P., *The Situational Leader*, Prentice-Hall, 1986.

Herzberg, F., 'One More Time: How Do You Motivate Employees?', *Harvard Business Review*, vol. 46, no. 1, 1968, pp. 53–62.

Hofstede, G., *Culture's Consequences: Comparing Values, Behaviors, Institutions and Organizations Across Nations*, Sage, 2003.

Ibarra, H., *Act Like a Leader, Think Like a Leader*, Harvard Business Review Press, 2015.

Janis, I.L., *Victims of Groupthink: A Psychological Study of Foreign-Policy Decisions and Fiascos*, Houghton Mifflin, 1982.

Jia, F., Gosling, J. and Witzel, M., *Sustainable Champions: How International Companies Are Changing the Face of Business in China*, Greenleaf, 2015.

Johns, C., *Becoming a Reflective Practitioner*, Wiley, 2025.

Joseph, S., *Authentic: How to Be Yourself and Why it Matters*, Piatkus, 2019.

Jurkiewicz, C.L. and Giacolone, R.A. (eds), *Radical Thoughts on Ethical Leadership*, Information Age Publishing, 2017.

Knights, D. and Willmott, H., *Introducing Organizational Behaviour and Management*, Cengage Learning, 2012.

Kotter, J., 'What Leaders Really Do', *Harvard Business Review*, vol. 68, no. 3, 1990, pp. 103–111.

Kraemer, H.M.J., *From Values to Action: The Four Principles of Value-Based Leadership*, Wiley, 2025.

Lazari-Radek, K. de and Singer, P., *Utilitarianism: A Very Short Introduction*, Oxford University Press, 2017.

Leigh, A., *Ethical Leadership: Creating and Sustaining an Ethical Business Culture*, Kogan Page, 2015.

Lewin, K., Lippitt, R. and White, R.K., 'Patterns of Aggressive Behavior in Experimentally Created "Social Climates"', *Journal of Social Psychology*, vol. 10, no. 2, 1939, pp. 269–299.

Lewis, J.S., *Partnership for All*, Kerr-Cros Publishing, 1948.
Machiavelli, N., *The Prince*, trans. T. Parks, Penguin, 2011.
Maio, G.R., *The Psychology of Human Values*, Routledge, 2016.
McChrystal, S., Collins, T., Silverman, D. and Fussell, C., *Team of Teams: New Rules of Engagement for a Complex World*, Penguin, 2015.
McIntosh, G.L. and Rima, S.D., *Overcoming the Dark Side of Leadership: How to Become an Effective Leader by Confronting Potential Failures*, Baker Books, 2007.
McQuade, A., *Ethical Leadership: Moral Decision-Making Under Pressure*, De Gruyter, 2022.
Mill, J.S. and Bentham, J., *Utilitarianism and Other Essays*, Penguin, 2000.
Nayak, A., 'Wisdom and the Tragic Question: Moral Learning and Emotional Perception in Organisations', *Journal of Business Ethics*, vol. 137, no. 1, 2016, pp. 1–13.
Obolensky, N., *Complex Adaptive Leadership: Embracing Paradox and Uncertainty*, Routledge, 2024.
Ohmae, K., *The Mind of the Strategist: The Art of Japanese Business*, McGraw-Hill, 1991.
Pasmore, W.A., *Designing Effective Organizations: The Sociotechnical Systems Perspective*, Wiley, 1988.
Peter, L.J. and Hull, R., *The Peter Principle: Why Things Always Go Wrong*, William Morrow, 1969.
Rawls, J., *A Theory of Justice*, Harvard University Press, 1999.
Riggio, R.E., Chaleff, I. and Lipman-Blumen, J. (eds), *The Art of Followership: How Great Followers Create Great Leaders and Organizations*, Jossey-Bass, 2008.
Rousseau, D.M., *Psychological Contracts in Organizations: Understanding Written and Unwritten Agreements*, Sage, 1995.
Schein, E.H., *Organizational Culture and Leadership*, Jossey-Bass, 2016.
Simon, H.A., *The Sciences of the Artificial*, MIT Press, 1996.
Stacey, R.D. and Mowles, C., *Strategic Management and Organisational Dynamics: The Challenge of Complexity to Ways of Thinking About Organisations*, Pearson, 2015.
Steiner, I.D., *Group Process and Productivity*, Academic Press, 1972.
White, A., *From Comfort Zone to Performance Management*, White & MacLean, 2009.
Witzel, M., Bolden, R. and Linacre, N., *Leadership Paradoxes*, Routledge, 2017.
Witzel, M., *Tata: The Evolution of a Corporate Brand*, Penguin India, 2009.
Witzel, M., *The Ethical Leader*, Bloomsbury, 2019.
Wu, G., *Between Deontology and Justice: Chinese and Western Perspectives*, trans. Li, Y., Zheng, Z. and Li, J., Routledge, 2019.

ACKNOWLEDGEMENTS

Writing a book can feel like a solitary process, but in reality, in writing as in leadership, nothing could be achieved without the rest of the team. My thanks go to Sarah Rae, my endlessly patient editor at Routledge, for allowing me the time to get over my own struggles and write this book. Megan Hiatt, the production editor, has made the latter stages of the process seem painless, and Liz Ottosson did a thorough and sympathetic job of copy-editing my manuscript, saving me from some egregious errors. Any mistakes that remain are of course my own responsibility.

A book like this does not come in a moment. I have been writing and teaching about leadership for many years now, and my influences during that time have been too numerous to mention. Rather than listing names, I would like to thank three groups. The first is the Fellowship Network of the Exeter Centre for Leadership along with my fellow critical friends in the Exeter Leadership Partners. Your ideas and thoughts from such a wide range of backgrounds have been endless stimulating, and I am proud and pleased to call so many of you my friends.

The second group is my students past and present on the MBA and Senior Leader Apprentice programmes at the University of Exeter Business School. For me, you have been a combination of laboratory where I could test my own ideas, and a fountain of knowledge and inspiration that has allowed me a look into the real lives of leaders. Without you, this book could not have been written.

Third, I would like to thank the anonymous reviewers of both the proposal and the completed manuscript. Your comments have been generous, supportive and critical all at the same time and helped me ensure that I stayed on the right track.

Morgen Witzel
2026

INDEX

For Product Safety Concerns and Information please contact our EU representative GPSR@taylorandfrancis.com
Taylor & Francis Verlag GmbH, Kaufingerstraße 24, 80331 München, Germany

www.ingramcontent.com/pod-product-compliance
Lightning Source LLC
LaVergne TN
LVHW010258060926
847296LV00047B/343
9781032802848